PENGUIN
IS YOUR CHILD READY

Professor Anupam Sibal (MD, FIMSA, FIAP, FRCP [Glasgow], FRCP [London], FRCPCH, FAAP) has been a paediatrician for twenty years. Trained in India and the UK, he helped set up the first successful paediatric liver transplant programme in India at Apollo Hospitals, Delhi, in 1998. Prof. Sibal has been the Group Medical Director of the Apollo Hospitals Group since 2005.

Prof. Sibal is an Honorary Clinical Professor at Macquarie University, Sydney, Australia. He has ninety-five publications in medical literature, serves on the editorial board of three journals and has edited a textbook of paediatric gastroenterology and hepatology.

Prof. Sibal lives in New Delhi with his wife, Nandini, and son, Devaang. This is his first non-medical book.

ADVANCE PRAISE FOR THE BOOK

'As parents, we carry the hopes and wishes of generations with the idea that our children will have better opportunities than we did. But let's face it, kids don't come with a manual. Prof. Sibal's book, which is beautifully thought-out and fashioned, is the manual that parents need. This book, which attests to his years as a father and paediatrician, should be mandatory reading for all parents.'

—Madhuri Dixit Nene, actress, and Dr Shriram Nene, cardiac surgeon

'Good deeds speak for themselves; the tongue only interprets their eloquence. A brilliant book with gripping stories that will enthral you. A must-have for every parent.'

—Navjot Singh Sidhu, former cricketer

'What we put into our children's minds today is what they are going to put back into the world tomorrow. As parents of a daughter, Romi and I both feel that what children learnt most naturally in the previous generations now requires a more concerted effort owing to the drastic change in the structure of our families and, consequently, the upbringing of our children. A great book by Prof. Anupam Sibal on a subject that parents need most help with today!'

—Romi and Kapil Dev, former cricketer

'As a cricketer, it is all about "another win"; as a batsman it is all about "another hundred". And then, 1 May 2014, Aazeen came into Natasha's and my life. Since then both the cricketer and the batsman have been "retired hurt" and life is all about another vaccination or another blanket when Aazeen is sleeping or another round of shopping at the Duty Free. Natasha says I will spoil her. While I wouldn't like to agree with her, deep down I know she is right. I say only "Yes" to Aazeen. Prof. Sibal's book will tell me how to draw a balance and teach me how to say "No" at times.'

—Gautam Gambhir, cricketer

'"More is caught than taught" as the saying goes, and Prof. Sibal demonstrates this important principle through a simple communication technique he's discerned from working with hundreds of children. Particularly powerful are the various stories he shares to teach important values to his own child—a chance for you

to repurpose (hack!) them for your own use, saving you hours and hours of time.'
—Verne Harnish, CEO, Gazelles, author of *Scaling Up* (*Rockefeller Habits 2.0*)

'It is said that while we are all descendants of our past, we are also the parents of the future. When a couple brings a child into the world, they are responsible, not just for the child, but also for how the child will influence the future of our world. My husband and I have been blessed with four wonderful daughters, all of them unique in their strengths and personalities. I think the one principle I have held in great regard is that our children learn more from what we are than from what we teach them. Above all, parenting is a great gift; it is an art as well as a labour of love. As Prof. Sibal has demonstrated in his well-written book, there is a science behind the art that can be learnt. This is a book that will serve as a boon for parents and even grandparents.'
—Sucharitha Reddy, author and culinary expert

'Prof. Sibal's inspiring writing lifted me up out of my daily corporate grind to remember that what makes life worth living and causes one to soar is what you do for your family and others, and what you do for humankind. That's where the big profit of life lies.'
—Jim Clifton, chairman and CEO, Gallup

'Every time I met Devaang with his father Prof. Sibal, I was pleasantly surprised with his brilliance, highly positive attitude, ambition coupled with politeness and respectfulness, and I always wondered, "How can one raise a child like that?" The secret was revealed when I read this book. What a great contribution to human development!'
—Dr Ashok K. Chauhan, founder president, Amity Global Education Group, and chairman, AKC Group of Companies

'Prof. Anupam Sibal, as felicitous a writer as any that I have encountered during my long journalistic career, has come out with a timely, topical and much-needed book. Prof. Sibal has captured with acuity the zeitgeist of our bewildering era, and his narrative thread asks: "Is there anyone more precious than one's child?" His book lays out a full road map for parents, would-be parents and children. It's a book replete with fundamental and enduring values, and is written with such superb foresight that it will always be read, regardless of the velocity of change. Prof. Sibal's training as a paediatrician supports his writing skills—he knows the subject very well indeed, and you would do well to read his book. I promise that you will re-read it, and I predict that you will keep returning to it.'

—Pranay Gupte, author and columnist

'Helping your child grow up into a good human being must count among the greatest joys in the world. And if you are a parent, you know it's not always an easy task. Luckily, help is at hand now as Prof. Sibal draws on his experience as a paediatrician and a parent to give you a hands-on guide to instilling the right values in your child. This is a book filled with fascinating stories, nuggets of wisdom and practical advice. Do your child a favour . . . no, do yourself a favour. Read this book!'

—Prakash Iyer, author and leadership coach

'We need two kinds of education—one that teaches us how to make a living and one that teaches us how to live. Every experience that Prof. Sibal has shared in his book teaches us how to live. This beautiful collection of living values resonates with a vibration of conviction and truth which radiates the inspiration to go back to being who we originally are. This book is for the child within each of us. Let us all be what we wish our children to be. The book not only inspires us to live our values but shares creative ways of making it an enjoyable experience for children so that they grow up believing that living by values is the only way to live.'

—Brahma Kumari Shivani

'His Holiness Pramukh Swami Maharaj, creator of Swaminarayan Akshardham, always says, "A family that eats together, plays together and prays together will stay together." Actively spending time together is bound to bring and keep a family together. It is through mutual understanding and active communication between parents and children that family bonds can remain strong and tight. This book wonderfully demonstrates that delicate but essential synergy is needed between parents and children. Prayers and best wishes for this book's author and readers.'

—Sadhu Gnanmunidas, senior swamiji, Swaminarayan Akshardham Mandir

Is Your
Child Ready
to Face the
World?

DR ANUPAM SIBAL

PENGUIN BOOKS

An imprint of Penguin Random House

PENGUIN BOOKS

USA | Canada | UK | Ireland | Australia
New Zealand | India | South Africa | China

Penguin Books is part of the Penguin Random House group of companies
whose addresses can be found at global.penguinrandomhouse.com

Published by Penguin Random House India Pvt. Ltd
7th Floor, Infinity Tower C, DLF Cyber City,
Gurgaon 122 002, Haryana, India

Penguin
Random House
India

First published by Penguin Books India 2015

ISBN 9780143423140

Typeset in Adobe Garamond Pro by Manipal Digital Systems, Manipal
Printed at Replika Press Pvt. Ltd, India

www.penguin.co.in

MIX
Paper from
responsible sources
FSC® C016779

To all the children I have had the privilege of caring for over the last two decades

Contents

Foreword

There are only two lasting bequests we can hope to give our children. One of these is roots, the other, wings. At the end of the day, the most overwhelming key to a child's success is the positive involvement of parents.

To be a good father and mother requires that the parents defer many of their own needs and desires in favour of the needs of their children. As a consequence of this sacrifice, conscientious parents develop a nobility of character and learn to put into practice the selfless truths.

Prof. Anupam Sibal, in this book, *Is Your Child Ready to Face the World?*, has, with great wisdom, compassion and experience, created a beautifully clear, comprehensive and practical (eighteen virtues and fifty dos and don'ts) guide for the type of mindful parenting parents could practise. Parents could think of it as an invitation to use the focus of their minds, and the compassionate love in their hearts, to raise happy children and find greater joy in parenting.

Ever so rarely, you come upon a book that is timeless. *Is Your Child Ready to Face the World?* will help one's whole family grow together through the ages.

Mumbai

8 October 2015   Amitabh Bachchan

Introduction

When it comes to being a father, it really doesn't matter whether you are the CEO of a Fortune 500 corporation, a sports star, an army officer, an engineer, a farmer or an information technology professional. For your child, you are just a father. Nothing more, nothing less.

When the announcement about the Nobel Peace Prize being awarded to President Obama was made, his daughter, Malia, went up to him and said, 'Daddy, you have won the Nobel Peace Prize, and it is Bo's birthday today' (Bo is the Portuguese water dog that the President gifted his daughters). Sasha, her younger sister, added, 'Plus, we have a three-day weekend coming up.' This goes to show that one could be president of the US and be awarded the Nobel Peace Prize, but for his daughters, he will just be 'Daddy', and all they will want to do is share the special day with him. For a child, being a child comes naturally. It is relatively simple. But for an adult to become a father, it is quite another story.

The thought of shouldering the huge responsibility of fatherhood can be daunting. For many fathers, meeting the material needs of their children—home, clothes, nutritious food, medical care and schooling—can be challenging. But beyond these, there is also a deep-rooted worry of failing as a father. Several questions haunt a man. Will my child be able to live up to the genetic potential with which he/she was born? Will I be able to instil in my child the values that I hold dear? Will my child learn to differentiate the good from the bad and follow the right path? Will he/she be a good human being, caring and kind? Will my child get along with people? Will he/she be successful and a responsible citizen? Will my child value family relationships, make a mark in his/her profession and leave the world a better place? The list of questions is endless. But, there is one underlying sentiment: Will I be able to discharge my duty as a father to prepare my child to face the world?

This sentiment was expressed by President Obama in a letter to his daughters when the family was moving into the White House. He wrote,

When I was a young man, I thought life was all about me—about how I'd make my way in the world, become successful, and get the things I want. But then the two of you came into my world. . . . And suddenly, all my big plans for myself didn't seem so important anymore. I soon found that the greatest joy in my life was the joy I saw in yours. And I realized that my own life wouldn't count for much unless I was able to ensure that you had every opportunity for happiness and fulfilment in yours. (Obama, 2009)

Roger Federer too shared his realization of this enormous responsibility: 'Before, I guess, Mum and Dad were everything, but now, in my case, I had two new girls, and all of a sudden, they are completely dependent on you, and there's a third generation' (Federer, 2009).

How does one prepare a child to face the world? Talking to one's child about the good and bad is one way. But most conversations end up being perceived as sermons. How does one communicate with a generation that just does not have the time to hear anyone, leave alone listen to them? Children, especially teenagers, just don't want to talk to their parents.

Give a child some excellent books, and hope and pray that they will be read. A lot of prayers are needed, as data shows that children don't really like to read any more. A study published in 2011 by the National Literacy Trust, UK, found that only three young people in ten read every day as a leisurely activity. More than a fifth of children and young people (22 per cent) rarely or never read unless they are forced to, more than half (54 per cent) prefer watching TV to reading and nearly a fifth (17 per cent) would be embarrassed if their friends saw them reading (Clark, 2012).

As a parent, sharing your experience so that your child doesn't make the same mistakes is another way of teaching them. Each one of us has so many stories to tell, so many incidents that we can relate to and so many lessons that we have learnt through experience, but one must remember Charles Wadsworth's words: 'By the time a man realizes that maybe his father was right, he usually has a son who thinks he's wrong.'

Over the years, based on my experience as a paediatrician, I have developed a method to communicate with our son. Over the last two decades, I have interacted with children and teenagers every day. I have spent hours observing how they interact with their parents. I have seen them passionately make a case declaring their independence. I have seen parents express their exacerbation when teenagers vociferously voice their opinions. I have sensed this desire from parents to figure out how to communicate with their children, to communicate effectively, seeking a meaningful interaction and a heart-to-heart conversation. Not every day, but at least sometimes. This opportunity to study the behaviour of children and adolescents, their interaction with their parents and how they relate to adults gave me the insights that I needed to develop this method. This book is an attempt to share my experiment.

As for my personal experience as a parent, I have always made it a point to try to get fifteen minutes of undivided attention from our son, Devaang. I would try to get this time with him when he wanted to; that was the challenge I took on. It would not be a fixed day every week or every other week, because this would have then become a formal activity, and that's something children and teenagers dislike; the very purpose would have been defeated. It could not be a sermon; it had to be a two-way conversation with me nudging him to talk about some recent incident. I would then dip into my limited repertoire of stories and incidents, and find an example that would fit in with the mood. Each story was structured in a way that it touched upon a value that I believed was important. Thankfully, the Internet was at hand to provide details that I needed. Often, he and I would together search the Web for more information, with him leading the way. Sometimes, we would spend an hour or even more. The moment he felt he wanted to stop, we would halt. After all, it had to be an activity that he felt he was driving.

I distinctly remember a few instances. As we raised our glasses—his glass of milk and my cup of tea—to salute Roger Federer as he lifted the US Open Cup, we talked about the power of gratitude. As tennis was the theme that day, we studied Arthur Ashe's amazing life. Another time, when he expressed a desire to buy an iPhone, I felt it would be a good time for him to learn about the highs and lows in the life of Steve Jobs. On 2 October, the birth anniversary of Mahatma Gandhi, we discussed how he changed the world. While we enjoyed the FIFA World Cup inaugural ceremony, Nelson Mandela's forgiveness became the topic of discussion. When I took Devaang to meet one of the greatest cricketers of all time, Sachin Tendulkar, we talked about humility.

What values did I choose? The values I believe that make ordinary men and women extraordinary. The values that humanity has known for millennia. The values that we all have read about and have tried to use as guiding principles for our lives. The values that are so attractive and so captivating, yet hard to make a part of everyday existence. The values that, without an iota of doubt, define greatness—humility, compassion, honesty, giving and forgiveness, among many others.

I tried to use my own experience frugally, being mindful of Mark Twain's words: 'When I was a boy of 14, my father was so ignorant I could hardly stand to have the old man around. But when I got to be 21, I was astonished at how much the old man had learned in seven years.' You might ask when a parent should ideally begin this engagement. As a paediatrician, I think it is an exercise that should commence around the age of twelve. There is sufficient intellectual development of the child by this age, and children are also more receptive than in their teenage years. Teenagers think they know everything. They believe that they should be giving advice and not getting it. You might wonder, 'Isn't twelve too late?' Not really, as a child needs to be mature to comprehend complex issues.

While the type of engagement I employed with our son cannot take place with a very young child, we should not forget that they start emulating their parents from a very early age, and it is thus important for parents to behave the way they expect their child to behave.

Children are remarkably perceptive. Their eyes closely observe, ears intently listen and minds keenly process what their environment has to offer. These experiences at a young age leave a lifelong impression. This is something parents should never forget. Jim Hansen said so rightly, 'They (your children) don't remember what you try to teach them. They remember what you are.'

I believe that I can provide only a father's perspective, regardless of however much I would like to say *parents'* point of view. But I cannot. A father cannot even come close to playing the role that a mother plays in a child's life. I have observed my wife Nandini's unconditional love for Devaang, the 24x7, 365 days a year routine of caring for him with a smile—the glow in her eyes when she saw him excel in school, and the tears when he was hospitalized. I have no choice but to place a mother on a much higher plane as a parent. As a father, I have tried my best to support her by instilling and reinforcing qualities that will help our child take on the challenge of adulthood.

Has my experiment with Devaang made a difference to his life? Hopefully, yes. I have no idea how he will turn out. I do, however, have the satisfaction of having tried—having tried to discharge my duty as a father to prepare him to face the world.

Through my years of fatherhood and when I began writing this book, I drew inspiration from Rudyard Kipling's poem 'If', and want it to spread the same message of hope that it lent me:

> If you can keep your head when all about you
> Are losing theirs and blaming it on you;
> If you can trust yourself when all men doubt you,
> But make allowance for their doubting too:
> If you can wait and not be tired by waiting,
> Or, being lied about, don't deal in lies,
> Or being hated don't give way to hating,
> And yet don't look too good, nor talk too wise;

> If you can dream and not make dreams your master;
> If you can think and not make thoughts your aim,
> If you can meet with Triumph and Disaster
> And treat those two impostors just the same.
> If you can bear to hear the truth you've spoken
> Twisted by knaves to make a trap for fools,
> Or watch the things you gave your life to, broken,

And stoop and build'em up with worn out tools;

If you can make one heap of all your winnings
And risk it on one turn of pitch and toss,
And lose, and start again at your beginnings.
And never breathe a word about your loss:
If you can force your heart and nerve and sinew,
To serve your turn long after they are gone.
And so hold on when there is nothing in you
Except the Will which says to them: 'Hold on!'

If you can talk with crowds and keep your virtue,
Or walk with Kings nor lose the common touch,
If neither foes nor loving friends can hurt you,
If all men count with you, but none too much.
If you can fill the unforgiving minute,
With sixty seconds' worth of distance run.
Yours is the Earth and everything that's in it,
And which is more, you'll be a Man, my son!

Humility

Do you wish to rise? Begin by descending. You plan a tower
that will pierce the clouds? Lay first the foundation of humility.

— Saint Augustine

Mahatma Gandhi regarded humility as an essential virtue
that ought to exist in an individual, before other virtues
emerge. Humility, he believed, was the starting point for
other virtues to be cultivated. Once, when he was travelling
by train to Porbandar, he encountered another passenger
who decided to occupy more room than his seat would allow.
He lay down on the seat, pushing Gandhi and even keeping
his feet on his lap. Although he caused much discomfort,
Gandhi chose not to react. As the train approached
Porbandar, the man announced that he was going to see
Mahatma Gandhi, not realizing that he had been with him
all night. As Gandhi alighted from the coach, he was greeted
by thousands of people who had come to the station to
welcome him. Realizing what he had done, the man fell at

Gandhi's feet. Gandhi, forever ready to forgive, smiled and told the man that he ought to be respectful towards every human being.

Sachin Tendulkar, regarded as the god of cricket by millions, is not only an exemplary cricketer but also a man with great virtues. In a country where cricket is like a religion, Tendulkar is virtually worshipped. He has numerous qualities that helped him to not only excel on the cricket field for twenty-four long years, but also win the hearts of millions across the world. One outstanding quality has been his humility. Hero worship and consistent performances could have let pride take over, but Tendulkar has remained the humble person he was when he first entered the international arena at the age of sixteen. Every child in India wants to meet Sachin Tendulkar, shake his hand and have a photograph clicked with him.

Hamza Akhtar, a six-year-old boy from Pakistan who was referred to me for treatment, was just the same. Diagnosed with chronic liver failure, he needed a transplant. During clinical assessment, I always ask about a child's interests so as to get to know the child better. Hamza mentioned to me that he loved to play cricket and his father added that Hamza was a good player. Of late, because of the increasing jaundice and growing weakness, he had not been able to play cricket, but he remained glued to the television whenever a cricket match was being telecast.

Two days before his transplant, as I was doing my morning rounds, Hamza stopped me just as I was leaving his room. He said, 'Dr Sibal, may I make a request? Can I meet Sachin Tendulkar? I know the Indian cricket team is in Delhi to play a test match.' I did not know how to react. I just smiled and told him I would come back to meet him later in the day to talk about his request. Here was a child who was to undergo a liver transplant forty-eight hours later, an operation that has a success rate of 90 per cent. If Hamza were not to survive the transplant, I would be haunted by the thought that a child's wish had not been fulfilled.

I was at the same time acutely aware of the difficulty of meeting Hamza's request. I decided to give it my best shot. I went to the Feroz Shah Kotla Stadium and sent a request through the stadium's medical team to meet Dr Anjali Tendulkar, Sachin's wife, who is a paediatrician. Anjali readily agreed to meet me, and I shared Hamza's request. Anjali took my number and promised to call later in the day. A few hours later, she rang me up to say that Sachin would be happy to meet Hamza in his hotel room.

I went to Hamza's room and shared the wonderful news with him and his family. Devaang pleaded to come along. That night, Hamza, Devaang and I went to meet the 'God of Cricket'. Sachin and Anjali greeted us very warmly, and Sachin started chatting with Hamza, who had carried his bat and a tennis ball. I had assumed that Hamza wanted his bat and the ball autographed, but I was in for a surprise. Hamza asked Sachin if he could play cricket with him. Sachin smiled and said, 'Hamza, you bat, and I will bowl.' The 20,000-watt smile that lit up Hamza's face is unforgettable. So Sachin bowled and Hamza batted. This went on for more than half an hour till Hamza got tired and said that he wanted to rest. Sachin was willing to play with Hamza for as long as he wanted. The meeting ended with Sachin signing Hamza's bat and giving him some chocolates. That day, Sachin Tendulkar convinced me that he was worthy of the worship of his fans. He behaved like a friend, not a superstar. He was just someone who went out of his way to make sure Hamza had an excellent time.

Hamza is now sixteen years old and leads a normal life. I am sure he thinks about that evening in Sachin Tendulkar's suite often. So do Devaang and I.

Gautam Gambhir too holds Sachin Tendulkar in high esteem. I have known Gautam for many years. He supports the Gift a Life Foundation and pledged his organs to launch the organ donation initiative of the Apollo Hospitals Group. Gautam himself is a very unassuming and humble person. Speaking about Sachin, he says, 'His humility speaks volumes about his character. His humility makes him the kind of person he is' (PTI, 2013).

Kapil Dev, the man who led the Indian team to its first World Cup victory in 1983, is another epitome of humility. He has been very supportive of the Apollo Hospitals Group's campaign to spread awareness about liver diseases in children, and over the years, has championed many programmes. A few years ago, it happened that Kapil and I were travelling back from London on the same flight, and I was lucky to be sitting next to him. As we settled in, a member of the airline staff said, 'Kapil, you probably won't remember me, but nearly forty years ago we used to play cricket together for our school team.' Kapil recognized him immediately and hugged him. I could see his friend's eyes moisten because little had he expected that he would be greeted with such warmth. When we were airborne, I complimented Kapil on his humility. He merely brushed off my compliment and said, 'I am the same Kapil Dev I was when I started playing and will remain so till my last day.'

I had the privilege of meeting Ratan Tata once. I was informed one morning that he would be visiting a friend whose father was admitted in the Intensive Care Unit of Apollo Hospital, Delhi. We have a protocol to handle visits by very important people, and as a result, I asked Mr Tata's assistant how long he would like to stay and whether we needed to make any special arrangements. We were told that we did not need to prepare for Mr Tata's visit. I greeted Mr Tata as he came into the hospital lobby, took him to his friend and offered them an exclusive waiting room that is used when dignitaries visit the hospital. Mr Tata politely declined and said that he would be comfortable spending time in the common waiting room and there was absolutely no need for us to do anything out of the ordinary. After his meeting, he thanked us for looking after the patient and insisted that I should not take the trouble of seeing him off to his car. The most admired businessman in India walked into our hospital and charmed his way into the hearts of everyone with his simplicity, down-to-earth nature and humility. Thomas Carlyle once said, 'A great man shows his greatness by the way he treats little men.' That day, I met a great man.

When I reached home that evening, I told Devaang about my amazing experience. He had witnessed Sachin's humility, heard about Kapil Dev's and was now learning of Ratan Tata. 'How can they remain so humble?' was a question that was perplexing Devaang. 'How can they remain grounded when everyone places them on such a high pedestal?' he asked.

I replied, 'I guess the fact that they do not let their ego rule their mind makes them great. Many men and women become very successful but few achieve greatness. Humility is the differentiation, the icing on the cake. These remarkable men must constantly work towards keeping their ego in check. Try and remember that, Devaang.'

Dr Prathap C. Reddy is regarded as the architect of modern healthcare in India. After spending a decade in the US, he returned to India in 1978 when doctors working abroad did not want to do so. He established a busy practice as a cardiologist. As there were no facilities for cardiac surgery in India at that time, he used to send his patients to the US for surgeries. One of his patients died before he could raise the money needed for his surgery, leaving behind a widow and two young children.

It was at this point that Dr Reddy asked himself a question. If Indian doctors could excel overseas and provide the best care, why could they not provide such care in India if the best infrastructure and support teams were made available to them? That's when he decided to set up India's first corporate hospital in Madras (now Chennai). From a 150-bed hospital, the Apollo Hospitals Group has today grown to become one of Asia's largest integrated healthcare delivery systems.

I joined the Apollo Hospitals Group in 1997 to help set up the first paediatric liver transplant programme in India. I had read about Dr Reddy but had not had the opportunity to meet him before joining. In our first meeting, he came across as someone who wanted to and had the ability to change the way healthcare was delivered in the country. Ever so gracious, in the first few minutes he made me feel comfortable. The amazing motivator that he is, he made us believe that we could not only establish the first liver transplant programme but also bring it on a par with the best programmes in the world.

Renowned writer Pranay Gupte, who is the author of Dr Reddy's biography, *The Healer*, touches upon many of Dr Reddy's outstanding qualities. Humility is the one that stood out in our first meeting. Dr Reddy always stands up to greet whoever enters his office. It does not matter if it is a minister or a housekeeper, Dr Reddy always stands up. I noticed this habit in 1997, and eighteen years later, when Dr Reddy is eighty-two years old, I see him still sticking to it. A few years ago, Dr Reddy had a fall and fractured a couple of ribs. He was asked to rest, but as he loves his work so much, he decided to come to work. That day, when everyone entered his office, he apologized for not standing up, saying that he had been forbidden by his orthopaedic surgeon to exert himself. I make it a point to get Devaang to interact with Dr Reddy as often as possible so that he can observe humility at close quarters and imbibe it.

I must also credit the founder of Springdales School, Mrs Rajni Kumar, and the principal, Dr Jyoti Bose, for their efforts to instil the virtue of humility in students from a very young age. The students of primary school at Springdales are encouraged to clean their classrooms, the moral being that no task is small or lowly. They are given opportunities to interact with children who are not as fortunate. This includes cleanliness drives, helping out with home assignments and sharing books and toys.

When our son was fourteen, I asked him if he thought he was humble. 'Yes, Dad,' was the reply. 'That is excellent,'

I said. 'You might want to work on being more humble, though,' I urged him. 'You could be more humble too,' was the instant reply. Devaang and I decided that we would point out each other's interactions with people wherein we came across as being humble. This became an interesting exercise that we both looked forward to. Devaang tried really hard to excel. Sunday afternoons were usually spent at a movie hall. Devaang would make it a point to greet the security staff at the mall entrance and thank them after he had been frisked. He greeted the staff at the movie hall, the ushers and the attendants at the snack bar by addressing them by name. He had figured out that as everyone carried a name badge, addressing an individual by name got him a smile virtually every time as against a simple 'Good afternoon'. Each time I pointed out to Devaang that he was doing well, I could see the joy in his eyes. At his school, we were told by the security supervisor and helpers that Devaang would greet them warmly every day. Junior school students told us that he was friendly and did not try to be bossy. In a way, our little competition to be humble had rubbed off as a habit.

Dr Dinesh Singh, Vice Chancellor of Delhi University, in the course of his third anniversary speech, mentioned that Devaang was his first intern during his second year of college. The very first task assigned to him was to scrub the office washroom. Devaang's body language did not show any hint of unwillingness and he cleaned the washroom with sincerity without flinching, unlike most others who came after him. As I noticed the tears in Nandini's eyes at this revelation, I realized that our child had learnt the dignity of labour and importance of humility.

I sincerely hope that Devaang continues to be humble as he grows older and hopefully becomes successful. Success and pride can go hand in hand. It is, therefore, important that we introduce our children to the virtue of humility before they taste success and allow pride to take root. Francois Fenelon put it well when he said, 'Humility is not a grace that can be acquired in a few months: it is the work of a lifetime.' So, we need to start early. We need to remind ourselves that humility is needed for other virtues to emerge.

Humility is not thinking less of yourself, it's thinking of yourself less.

— C.S. Lewis

Beating the Odds

Success is not measured by what you accomplish, but by the opposition you have encountered, and the courage with which you have maintained the struggle against overwhelming odds.

— Orison Swett Marden

When we do not achieve what we had set out to achieve, we fall back on excuses to make ourselves feel better. We all may have used variants of:

> 'I would have achieved my goal, but luck was not on my side.'
> 'If only I had been given the resources I needed, I would have been successful.'
> 'My co-workers just could not see me succeed and pulled me down.'
> 'If only I had a family that understood that I needed the space to accomplish what I had set out to do.'

. . . and so on. When children see their parents make excuses, they tend to do the same.

Perhaps the most common scenario in which people make excuses is when it comes to staying fit. Over the last decade, I have seen a significant increase in the incidence of obesity among school children. After a detailed history, physical examination and investigations, obese children are advised to adhere to a diet plan and an exercise regimen. The dietary advice is usually relatively simple—decrease fats and carbohydrates, increase the intake of vegetables and have frequent small meals. So is the exercise regimen—exercise for forty-five minutes a day, six times a week, with brisk walking as a suggested mode of exercise. Often, children fail to adhere to the medical advice. The reasons range from the mushrooming of fast-food outlets to home delivery of junk food, increasing access to precooked meals and advertising of aerated beverages. Exercise is also often neglected with the excuses of paucity of time because of a hectic academic schedule, hot weather making exercise more difficult and lack of sports facilities. It is interesting to note that the excuses offered have little to do with what is actually expected from the child. Offering excuses is easier than making the changes. Children see their parents offer similar reasons for not losing weight (obesity does tend to run in some families) and they quickly ape their parents.

However, there are people who do not rely on excuses. In fact, they have succeeded even when the odds were stacked heavily against them.

Simi Singh joined my clinic as clinic manager in 2003. Simi had the most amazing smile, and she was exceptionally gifted in her people skills. Soon, she became rather popular with the kids and their mothers. Within two weeks of Simi's arrival, Nandini saw several changes in the clinic. The way the toys and games were displayed, little smileys on the files of the children, a new neatly created birthday list and an efficient system of arranging files were just some of the improvements. Simi brought a smile to everyone who visited the clinic with her charm, conquering even the tough task of making worried mothers smile. Working with Simi, our family, and especially Devaang, gained insight into what it means to overcome odds.

Simi was a teenager when she developed rheumatoid arthritis, an inflammatory condition of the joints. Despite anti-inflammatory medication, her symptoms worsened. The potency of the medication was increased but her condition continued to worsen. Her joint mobility was seriously compromised, and she needed four joint replacements by the time she turned twenty-one. Over the next three years, she started having unbearable pain in other joints of the body. However, no one who met Simi had any idea about her serious medical condition, her numerous surgeries and her dependence on multiple medications to keep her relatively pain-free and mobile. Despite numerous challenges, Simi is one of the most cheerful people I know and is always ready with a smile.

The fighter that Simi is, she once told me, 'In my heart of hearts, I knew that I had to stand up for myself. People can only sympathize with me, but it was I who would have to show negativity the "exit" sign and open doors for positivity.'

Throughout history, there have been amazing women and men who have overcome odds that seem insurmountable. When I come across children trying to make excuses, I often use the example of Ludwig van Beethoven, especially if the child is interested in music.

One of the most influential composers of Western classical music, Ludwig van Beethoven showed keen interest in music from an early age, and by his early twenties, had become a popular musician. At the age of twenty-six, he developed tinnitus. Tinnitus is a condition in which a person perceives a ringing sound in the ear that makes hearing problematic. Beethoven initially lost the ability to hear higher frequencies. Later, the hearing loss became more pronounced, and he could not even hear the audience applaud. By the age of thirty-four, Beethoven was almost deaf. Did Beethoven use his hearing disability as an excuse? On the contrary, a majority of his most-celebrated works were composed after he developed the hearing disability. The ninth symphony, the last five piano sonatas and the last five string quartets were composed when he was almost deaf.

When the war against polio in India reached its final phase, there was a lot of media time and space devoted to polio. Devaang and I talked about Franklin D. Roosevelt, who at thirty-nine was afflicted with polio. He lost the use of his legs and was confined to a wheelchair. But he overcame the depression that resulted from this permanent disability and became governor of New York. At fifty-one, he became the president of the US. He was the only president in the history of the US to have served for more than two terms.

Roosevelt founded the National Foundation for Infantile Paralysis (NFIP) to help develop a vaccine against polio. NFIP supported a polio research project steered by Dr Albert Sabin.

This foundation appointed Dr Jonas Salk to develop a polio vaccine. In 1959, Dr Salk's 'killed' polio virus became the first successful polio vaccine. In 1962, Dr Sabin developed the 'oral' polio vaccine. By 2014, polio had been eradicated in all but three countries. Roosevelt's vision helped rid the world of polio, showing that often one man's dream is enough.

Every time Devaang and I watch a Steven Spielberg movie, I like to bring up the fact that Spielberg not only did his best to overcome the obstacles in his way, but also actively pursued his dream in his own time. A winner of three Academy Awards, he has films like *Lost Ark*, *Indiana Jones and the Kingdom of the Crystal Skull*, *Jaws*, *ET* and *Jurassic Park* to his name. In school, Steven Spielberg's grades were average as he had dyslexia. Therefore, he was unable to gain admission into a film school. His love for filmmaking drew him to Universal Studios in Los Angeles, where he would spend three days a week observing professionals, talking to them and asking them questions. He thus became a self-trained filmmaker. In 2005, *Empire Magazine* declared Spielberg as the greatest film director of all time. He has famously said, 'I do not dream at night. I dream all day. I dream for a living.'

In 2011, Matt Stutzman set a Guinness World record for the longest accurate shot. What makes his record outstanding is the fact that he has no arms. His adopted parents instilled in his mind the belief that 'impossible is a state of mind'. Stutzman learnt to do everything using his feet, including eating, driving, playing the guitar and fishing. In the 2012 London Paralympic games, he won a silver medal in archery. He has a special technique to load arrows with his feet. After he won the award, he said in an interview with *Perth Now*,

'My goal was to inspire somebody, even if it was just one person, with my positive attitude. Never say never! If I can do this, with no arms, anything is possible. Watching me people can only say, "I haven't got an excuse. I can't say my back's hurting or I got a sore finger, this guy's shooting arrows with no arms." I hope I make everyone realize you can do whatever you want in this life if you just try' (Foreman, 2012).

We also have to teach our children that sometimes clear paths are suddenly interrupted by seemingly insurmountable barriers, but it is at these moments that they must be most resilient. To my young patients who come up with the most innovative excuses and blame their luck for having a certain condition, I often like to quote the example of Jean Dominique Bauby, a respected French journalist who used to be the editor of *Elle*. At forty-three, he suffered a massive stroke and was in a coma. Three weeks later, he woke up but was in a locked-in syndrome. In this condition, while the mental state is normal, the body lies in a state of paralysis. Bauby could not speak and lost the ability to use his upper and lower limbs. The only movement he had control over was the ability to move his left eyelid. He learnt how to communicate through the technique of partner-assisted scanning. Whenever the interlocutor stopped at the desired letter, he would blink. Through this method, he wrote a book *The Diving Bell and the Butterfly*. Thus, the entire book was conceived, written and edited one letter at a time, relying entirely on the blinking of the left eyelid!

Next time we feel like making an excuse, or our children start going down the excuse route, we perhaps need to think and talk about Beethoven's deafness, Roosevelt's polio, Spielberg's dyslexia and Bauby's locked-in syndrome. Children also learn well if they can draw inspiration from the lives of people they know well, someone who has overcome numerous challenges—someone as brave as Simi. This way, there will be no excuse to come up with an excuse.

I had all of the disadvantages required for success.

— Larry Ellison

It's Never Too Late

Nobody can go back and start a new beginning, but anyone can start today and make a new ending.

— Maria Robinson

Watching a television programme on the Nobel Prize winners for 2010, I asked Devaang, 'What do Theodore Roosevelt, Thomas Woodrow Wilson, Alfred Schweitzer, Dr Martin Luther King Jr, Mother Teresa, Desmond Tutu, the fourteenth Dalai Lama, Nelson Mandela and Barack Obama have in common?' Devaang was quick to respond: 'Dad, as this question has been posed while we are watching a programme on Nobel Prize Winners, I guess the answer is that they all have won the Nobel Prize.' I replied, 'Correction. They all made immense contributions to the world and won the Nobel Peace Prize. Theodore Roosevelt, Thomas Woodrow Wilson, Nelson Mandela and Barack Obama led nations. Dr Martin Luther King Jr, Desmond Tutu and Nelson Mandela led their people to emancipation. Albert Schweitzer left his country to help people in Africa. The fourteenth Dalai Lama and Mother Teresa did not let geographical boundaries restrict them from spreading their message of compassion and love.' 'Do you know the interesting story about the origin of the Nobel Prize?' I asked. 'What could be so interesting?' was the instant response.

Alfred Nobel was born in Sweden. He was a trained chemist and also a linguist. He filed his first patent for a gas meter when he was twenty-four. Soon, he started experimenting with explosives and devoted himself to the study of nitroglycerine. He invented a detonator, the 'Nobel lighter' and a blasting cap. Nobel's factory where he was experimenting with nitroglycerine blew up. Five people, including his younger brother, were killed in the explosion. However, this explosion and several other accidents did not deter him but only strengthened his resolve to develop more stable explosives. In 1867, he invented dynamite by mixing nitroglycerine with diatomaceous earth. While he thought of calling it 'Nobel's Safety Powder'—to highlight its safety—he eventually decided to call it dynamite, alluding to the ancient Greek word for power, *dynamis*.

Dynamite revolutionized several industries. Mining and construction companies benefitted substantially. It was used by companies to blast through difficult terrain to create roads and railroads. Dynamite soon found its way into armaments and began to be used extensively in warfare. While Nobel realized the immense destructive power of dynamite, he believed dynamite could bring about everlasting peace. He once said to the peace advocate, Bertha Von Suther, 'My factories may make an end of war sooner than your congresses.

The day when two army corps can annihilate each other in one second, all civilized nations, it is hoped, will recoil from war and discharge their troops' (Odelberg, 1972).

Nobel continued his experiments and invented gelignite and ballistite. At one time, he had 355 patents to his credit.

In 1888, his brother, Ludvig, died, and a French newspaper mistakenly printed Alfred Nobel's obituary. The newspaper wrote '*Le marchand de la mort est mort*', meaning 'The merchant of death is dead'. Alfred was described as a man 'who became rich by finding ways to kill more people faster than ever before' (Hiskey, 2011).

This incident had a profound effect on Nobel. He started thinking about how to change his legacy. After much deliberation, he wrote his last will and testament, leaving approximately 94 per cent of his wealth to the establishment of five prizes: Physics, Chemistry, Physiology or Medicine, Literature and Peace. The prizes were to go to '. . . those who, during the preceding year, shall have conferred the greatest benefit to mankind', he wrote (www.nobelprize. org). USD 2.69 million was allocated for this purpose. Five years after his death, in 1901, the first set of Nobel Prizes were awarded.

Doctors eagerly await the news about the greatest recognition that any medical scientist or doctor can aspire for—the Nobel Prize in Physiology and Medicine. Dr Joseph E. Murray and Dr E. Donnall Thomas received the Nobel Prize in Physiology and Medicine in 1989 for their immense contribution to organ and cell transplantation. Their novel work transformed our understanding of the rejection of transplanted organs and paved the way for the development of anti-rejection medication, which has resulted in survival rates of more than 90 per cent for most organ transplants. I see the result of their work in the smiling faces of children who have had a successful liver transplant and are now leading a normal life. This is just one example of the impact of the work of the recipients of one Nobel Prize. There are hundreds of such examples.

What if Nobel had not read that obituary? What if after reading that obituary and realizing what others thought of his invention and its impact, he had done nothing to change his legacy? He would have been remembered as the inventor of dynamite, which, although revolutionized several industries and benefitted mankind, also caused innumerable deaths. But today, he is remembered for the Nobel Prizes. He has transcended from war to peace.

It is important to introduce children to the idea of a legacy early on. But how do you explain this concept to a twelve-year-old or a teenager who thinks a legacy is left behind only by older people? Often, as parents, we are so caught up in making sure that our children excel at the task at hand or in teaching them about how to act in a current situation that this aspect gets neglected. When I told Devaang about Alfred Nobel's story and the attempt he made, it got him thinking about his own life and how he wanted to contribute to the world. Thus, after the topic had been introduced in a way that was interesting for him and at the same time inspirational, the discussion took off in the direction of imagining how he would be remembered.

Planting the seed for the desire to have an admirable legacy to leave behind is something that sustains itself. It hardly requires reinforcing through multiple instances and lessons, and children feed off this desire. It moulds their actions and mindset to constantly do better, become more proficient and thus be able to leave an indelible mark on the world. Acting as an overarching goal they can work towards, it gives their actions a sense of purpose. Also, because it is not a fixed, defined goal—like scoring 90 per cent on an exam—it can change and grow over time according to a child's changing inclinations, likes and dislikes.

On the other hand, we also need to make sure that the thought of a legacy does not become a burden or pressure that our children cannot cope with. As parents, we need to reassure them that creating a legacy takes time. Even if they go wrong or do not see results in the field or activity they set to master, they must be reminded that it's never too late to create an impact. The very fact that they seek to do something great is a victory for us. Always at the backdrop of our guidance must be the idea that virtues make a person great.

Often, adults tell each other that it is too late; they could have done this or that but now the time and opportunity has passed. We should refrain from such an attitude, because when our children hear us say this, they start echoing us. If we cannot believe in what we are telling them, why should they? What needs to be done instead is to highlight that each day, week, month and year comes with unlimited opportunities and that it is never too late to seize those opportunities.

One day your life will flash before your eyes. Make sure it's worth watching.

— Gerard Way

Courage

Courage is the capacity to confront what can be imagined.

— Leo Rosten

In 2005, one of Devaang's friends was diagnosed with juvenile diabetes. This form of diabetes is insulin-dependent. Given that insulin is only available in injectable forms, this diagnosis translates to lifelong dependence on injections of insulin. When Devaang learnt that his friend would initially need not only up to four injections a day, but also a lifetime of diet restrictions, a regulated lifestyle, the need to carry insulin at all times, regular blood tests and consultations with not just endocrinologists but also other specialists, he was really upset. Life changes dramatically once a diagnosis is made. Devaang was very concerned about how his fourteen-year-old friend would cope. 'What about his family, his sister? How will they make the numerous changes that would need to be made?' he asked. In a few weeks, Devaang shared the good news that his friend was feeling great, the injections were not such a pain and the restrictions not so hard to adhere to. I took this as opportunity to reiterate to Devaang why facing challenges with a smile is exemplary courage.

I told him that every week in my practice, I see children who display extraordinary courage. Thalassemia patients, being on a pump every night to remove extra iron (because of repeated blood transfusions), are heroic. Children with Hepatitis B and C, coping with repeated blood tests and injections, are courageous. His own cousin, Dhiren, who took a growth hormone injection every day for years, was an excellent example.

Using an example Devaang could relate to easily, I said, 'Your hero, Marc Zuckerberg, displayed courage by dropping out of Harvard, a university that thousands would do anything to get into. He believed he could create a company that could change the way people relate to each other. Facebook did exactly that. Jeff Bezos quit a comfortable job in a hedge fund to start Amazon in a garage. Bezos based his decision on whether he would regret the decision when he was eighty and looking back at life. By quitting his job, he displayed courage.'

I urged Devaang to find out about people who had put everything at stake to achieve their next goal when they were already successful. 'Risking everything when you have made it big . . . Dad, that would be silly, wouldn't it?' was Devaang's view. 'It might be considered foolish,' I said, 'but then, these remarkable people displayed rare courage to achieve what they believed in.' I decided to tell our son about two of my medical heroes, Dr Christiaan Barnard and Dr Thomas Starzl.

Barnard was not only a brilliant surgeon, but also an able researcher. As a surgical trainee, he began to research a condition called congenial duodenal atresia, wherein the part of the intestine adjoining the stomach does not develop in babies. The babies begin vomiting after birth, and the treatment is a surgical procedure. Barnard observed that the success rate following surgery was poor. He examined different explanations for what caused the disease and the reasons why surgery wasn't a very successful option. He discovered that poor blood supply to that region of the small intestine was to blame. The reason surgeries were not successful was because they did not account for this. Barnard propagated a revised procedure that entailed more extensive removal of the intestine, and the results improved dramatically.

As a child, Barnard had seen his brother die at the age of five due to an untreatable heart condition. Thus, early on in his career, he was also driven to develop ways to treat untreatable heart diseases. He developed new techniques to cure heart diseases in children, creating a new valve to treat valvular disease. Barnard believed that anything others could do, he could as well. He continued to find ways to make cardiac surgery more successful and safe. He also started thinking about heart transplantation, preparing for it by performing kidney transplants.

In 1967, Louis Washkansky was referred to Dr Barnard with incurable heart disease and was likely to survive only for a short period of time. On 2 December 1967, Barnard received a call informing him that a lady called Denise Darvall had met with an accident and her family had agreed to donate her heart. Opportunity had come knocking, and he was faced with many questions. Should he embark on a procedure that had never been undertaken before? Was he ready? Was the team well prepared? Surgeons in other countries had done more work on animals. Should he do more animal work before doing a transplant in a human? Finally he threw caution to the wind and decided to take up the challenge.

He took Denise to the operation theatre, took out her heart and connected it to the heart lung machine. He removed Louis's heart and replaced it with Denise's heart. The thirty-member team took nine hours to perform the operation. Louis recovered and Barnard became world famous. However, nineteen days later, Louis developed pneumonia and succumbed to it.

Four weeks later, an opportunity arose for another heart transplant. Barnard knew that if this patient died as well, heart transplantation would forever be tinted with apprehension. He had a choice. He could bask in the glory of the first successful albeit short-lived heart transplant and wait till overall understanding of transplantation improved, or he could risk everything and go ahead with the second heart transplant. He chose the latter.

The second heart transplant was performed on 2 January 1968, and the patient, Philip Blaberg, lived for nineteen months and fifteen days. Barnard's courage paved the way for the establishment of heart transplantation. His work also set the stage for defining brain death criteria. This resulted in organ transplantation becoming standard therapy for end-stage organ failure. Barnard's surgery was emulated by surgeons across the globe. According to him, 'You learn from mistakes, but success gives you the courage to go on and do even more.' He continued to innovate and performed many more heart and lung transplants.

Barnard was not only a pioneer in the field of medicine, but he also opposed apartheid by allowing mixed-race nurses in the operation theatre and transplanting the heart of a white woman into a black man. Each year, 4,000 people worldwide undergo a heart transplant. They all have Christiaan Barnard to thank. When one looks back at Barnard's life, one realizes that he started making bold and courageous decisions early in life, a lesson that is important for parents trying to instil confidence in their children.

Thomas Starzl's mother, who was a nurse, inspired him to become a doctor. After training as a surgeon, Starzl started his experiments by performing liver transplants in animals. After working in Miami and Chicago, he moved to Colorado to practise as a surgeon, while engaging in transplant research. After five years of research, he attempted a human liver transplant in a three-year-old boy who died from bleeding. Two months later, he attempted another liver transplant in an adult, and the patient died three weeks later.

Faced with failure, he suspended human liver transplantation and started working on controlling bleeding and decreasing the risk of rejection of the transplanted organ. He realized that he would have to perfect transplantation in a less complex organ such as the kidney. So that became his new goal. Using steroids and another medicine (azathioprine) to control rejection of the kidney by the recipient, he and his team met with success. Starzl then started working on a more potent immunosuppressive (anti-rejection medicine) called cyclosporine.

In 1967, he believed he was ready again to perform a liver transplant in a human. By then, he was well established as a kidney transplant surgeon and his research in transplantation was widely respected. Not content, he decided to pursue liver transplantation. There was much to lose. His earlier attempts had failed on more than one occasion, and his reputation was at stake. That year, he performed the first successful liver transplant in an adult. Over the next thirteen years, his team performed 200 liver and 1,000 kidney transplants. More than 20,000 people across the world undergo a liver transplant each year, largely because of Thomas Starzl's work.

When the Apollo Hospitals Group was celebrating the tenth anniversary of successful liver transplantation in India in 2008, we invited Dr Starzl to be the chief guest. After all, who could have been more appropriate for the occasion? Dr Starzl expressed his inability to travel due to advancing age, but never one to not go the extra mile, he recorded and sent a video wishing us the best for the future.

Thousands of patients are able to lead normal lives today thanks to path-breaking work by these remarkable doctors. The Japanese Liver Transplantation Society Registry in 2013 reported close to 80 per cent survival for twenty years after liver transplantation (Kasahara et al., 2013). This would have been unimaginable three decades ago. But then Dr Christiaan Barnard and Dr Thomas Starzl changed the face of procedures and redefined the boundaries of medicine. They did that through a rare display of courage, risking their reputation and careers because they believed they could make a huge difference to the lives of patients with organ failure.

When I recounted all of this to Devaang, I was really pleased to see him engrossed in the stories. I could see that they had made him stop and reconsider the importance of courage. His next question proved it: 'These are indeed remarkable stories of courage. Tell me, how can children be courageous?' I told him that standing up for what you believe is right, standing by a classmate who wants to do the right but unpopular thing, questioning what others might take as granted are all examples of courage. Responding to failure in academics and sports not by running away but by doing better the next time is courage. I told our son, 'Little acts of courage over a period of time can give you the confidence to be really brave and achieve things on the same scale as Dr Christiaan Barnard and Dr Thomas Starzl. Such courage does not appear overnight, but takes conditioning.'

When Richard Branson was four years old, his mother would drop him off a few miles from their home. She wanted him to learn how to find his way home. When he was not yet twelve, she made him cycle to Bournemouth, a distance of 80 km. While she packed him sandwiches, she did not give him any water; she wanted him to fend for himself. She wanted him to be courageous. The lessons she taught him at a young age did yield impressive results. By the time he was sixteen, Branson had started his first business venture. At twenty-two, he had created Virgin records. When passengers enjoy the excellent service Virgin Airlines offers, they need to thank Richard Branson's mother for instilling in Branson the courage and ability to think out of the box.

When we see our children wanting to do something that we believe will be too hard to do or too risky, we tend to stop them because we do not want them to fail or to get hurt. But before we try and stop them, we need to pause and think. We should not let our own experience stand in the way of what they can learn. We need to let them be courageous to pursue what they want to. If they fail, they will learn from their failure. It they succeed, they might make the world a better place.

I learned that courage was not the absence of fear, but the triumph over it. The brave man is not he who does not feel afraid, but he who conquers that fear.

— Nelson Mandela

Handling Pressure

Get tough: don't work under pressure; work over pressure.

— Brian Celio

Till Devaang was in school (he is now twenty-two), Nandini and I looked forward to attending the annual day celebrations at his school. Watching the choir performances, plays and dances was always great fun. The evening would also provide us with an opportunity to interact with other parents. Of course, there was also a prize distribution ceremony. Virtually every annual day, the topic of performance would come up. Parents of the prize winners would be interested not just in how many prizes their children had won but also whether they had won the maximum number of prizes. Winning two prizes if someone else had won three was not good enough. Parents of children who had not won any would be visibly disappointed. I could visualize many children being told to work harder when they got home that night. The children who had not won the maximum number of prizes would be reminded that they could have done better. The child who had won the most prizes would be told to maintain this performance. Whether they acknowledged it or not, it was clear that parents were putting their children under tremendous pressure to perform.

I see children as young as five years old in my clinic who complain of pressure. Sometimes, it's the pressure to behave as a good girl or boy at all times or the pressure to excel in academics, and sometimes the pressure to attend music and dance classes. Then there's also the pressure to not just participate but also win, the pressure of meeting their parents' expectations at all times and, in many cases, the pressure to live the dreams of their parents.

This pressure can lead to physical symptoms in children. Headache, stomach pain and difficulty in sleeping are common manifestations. Functional abdominal pain is a common condition in children. In a study conducted by the Apollo Hospitals Group in two schools in south Delhi, it was found that 14 per cent of the 1,000 children interviewed had functional abdominal pain (Wadhwa and Sibal, 2007). In this disorder, children complain of vague abdominal pain that arises because of a dysregulation between the central and the enteric (intestinal) nervous system. Stressors can trigger the onset of this condition in many children. Arguments between parents, a serious illness or death within the family and change of school or residence are well-known stressors. Of late, I have found the pressure to perform a common trigger.

Once you get to know children well, they freely talk about this pressure. It is sometimes overt and sometime subtle, but there is pressure none the less. It is not just parents but also grandparents and the school who add to the pressure. If a child wins an interschool competition once, he or she is expected to win every time.

There is also considerable peer pressure that children face these days. I recently saw a fourteen-year-old boy who lost 10 kg over four months. Other than that, he had no symptoms and signs of any problem. Weight loss of this degree can be a marker of a serious disease, and understandably, the boy had seen several doctors, and a battery of tests had been performed. He had not been vomiting and/or throwing away food. Repeated questioning on why he was eating less had met with no clear response other than 'I just don't feel like eating more.' It was only during my second consultation that the father mentioned that the boy had been teased for being overweight by his classmates in the previous term. They used to call him 'golu' or 'round'. It was not that the boy was obese, just a tad bit on the heavier side, so the parents believed that he was not going to be affected by the teasing. However, the boy had taken the comments to heart. Not only did he eat less than before at home, he had virtually stopped eating during school hours. Snacks and lunch at school were given a miss. He gave them to his friends. He set himself the target of becoming thin. After a few sessions of counselling, he started eating better.

If we were to grade pressure, many of us would agree that, as a doctor, the pressure of saving lives would be rated as high pressure. Among medical professionals, there would be agreement that the pressure neurosurgeons face each time they operate is of the highest degree. A centimetre here instead of there can leave the patient paralysed.

I once had the opportunity of meeting a neurosurgeon, Dr Ben Carson, who handles pressure extremely well. A top paediatric neurosurgeon, he was once asked how he handled pressure, to which he replied, 'No matter how good you are at planning, the pressure never goes away. So, I don't fight it. I feed off it. I turn pressure into motivation to do my best.' As parents, it is our responsibility to not only *not* add to the pressure, but also talk to our children about handling pressure, as some amount of it is inevitable in day-to-day life.

I met Ben when he was invited to Apollo Hospital in Delhi, as we were planning a complex surgery to separate conjoined twins. These conjoined twins were fused at the head and shared complex anatomy. Our team felt that we should seek an expert opinion from Ben, who is perhaps the world's most famous paediatric neurosurgeon with an impressive track record of separating conjoined twins. After I wrote to Ben and we spoke a couple of times, he very graciously agreed to fly down to Delhi and brought along his charming wife, Lacena Rustin. He spent a couple of days with us assessing the twins and felt that separating them was possible.

While the operation did not take place as the family decided against the surgery, this consultation gave many of us an opportunity to learn about Ben's life.

Ben's mother Sonya had to juggle two to three jobs to make ends meet, as she had to provide for Ben and his brother by herself. He told us about how he wasn't a very good student at school initially and how his mother, Sonya, had to force him to read.

While reading had a profound effect on Ben and improved his grades, he continued to have a problem with his uncontrollable temper. The problem had begun when he was a weak student and his classmates would make fun of him for his poor performance. Even after his academic performance improved, he was often quick to flare up. He once disagreed with his mother over the choice of clothes and hit her with a hammer. Once, he argued with a friend over a choice of radio stations and, in a rage, stabbed him. Luckily, the pen knife snapped on the large belt buckle and prevented what could have been a fatal injury. Ben recounted this incident in an interview with Jarrod Stackelroth (Stackelroth, 2008).

Ben realized after the knife incident that he had a 'pathological' temper. He locked himself in the bathroom for three hours while reading the Book of Proverbs in the Bible and cried out to God to change his attitude. He found salvation in a passage that went, 'Better a patient man than a warrior, a man who controls his temper than one who takes a city.'

Ben also recounted how he had got a job and scholarship to get through college and become a neurosurgeon. He brought back a technique called a hemispherectomy, where one hemisphere, or one half, of the brain is completely removed. It would be hard to find a task that could come close to the pressure such an operation would place on a surgeon. The technique helped many children who suffered from severe and frequent seizures. Over the years, Ben has made the operation much safer through major surgical innovations.

In 1987, Ben created medical history by separating the Binder twins, who were joined at the back of the head. Separation of such twins is always fraught with danger and one twin, if not both, can die. The operation, which lasted twenty-two hours, was successful.

In 1997, he decided to take on the separation of the Banda boys in South Africa. As the twins shared major blood vessels in the back of their heads, this operation was particularly risky. The operation required extensive planning. To plan precisely for the operation, a 3D virtual computerized model was created, and Ben practised the steps of the surgery many times. Planning, team work and managing pressure worked well, and the team of fifty successfully managed the separation over twenty-eight hours.

But operations are not always successful.

The Iranian conjoined twins Ladan and Laleh Bijani died. Separation of adult conjoined twins had never been attempted before Ladan and Laleh. Ben knew that such an operation could kill or disable permanently either one or both of them. The risks in such cases are much higher as an adult brain does not have the same ability to reorganize as the brain of a child. Handling the pressure under the glare of the global media required extraordinary faith in his abilities and team.

In 2002, Ben had to face tremendous pressure—pressure of a different nature. He was diagnosed with prostate cancer and it appeared that the cancer had spread. Ben was shaken, but he accepted the disease with dignity. It did change his outlook on life:

> It gave me real perspective. . . . I remember the day after the MRI walking around my property and noticing so many things I had never noticed before. . . . [T]he beauty of the leaves on the trees, the blades of grass, and the

incredible symphonies put on by the birds that I had never listened to before. . . . I think I am even more empathetic now when people are facing death or when they are facing really horrible things, in terms of having a real sense of how they feel. So I think it was a good thing. (Lawton, 2008)

Imagine finding positivity in a diagnosis of cancer.

Having read about his calm approach to life in general and surgery in particular, I asked Ben if it was true that he didn't get angry. Wouldn't he get angry when things in the operation theatre were not the way he would like them to be or when things did not go the way they should? Didn't the constant pressure get to him? He said the last time he had gotten angry was when he had nearly knifed his friend. His wife agreed.

Ben Carson has not only perfected the art and science of neurosurgery, he has perfected something a lot more difficult: controlling anger and managing pressure.

The thing about pressure is how one approaches and deals with it. I particularly like what Sadhu Gnanmunidas, senior Swamiji of Akshardham temple, told us at a discourse held at Apollo Hospital, Delhi, in 2013. An acting president was visiting the Akshardham Temple, and he wanted to know how he could handle the intense pressure of running a nation better. Sadhu Gnanmunidas replied, 'When you carry a pitcher of water on your head, you feel a lot of pressure because you believe you are carrying the load. In contrast, when you go diving, you do not feel the pressure of gallons of water above your head. This is because you do not believe you are carrying the load. So, President, stop thinking that you are carrying the load, and the pressure will go away.'

As parents, what can we do about pressure on our children? Firstly, we should not add to the pressure by focusing only on performance. Secondly, we should avoid the temptation of comparing our children with others. There is enough peer pressure anyway. Thirdly, we should ask our children about whether they feel they are under undue pressure or not. If they say that they are, we should then ask them about what we can do to reduce the pressure they face and help them deal with it. How we cope with pressure will have considerable bearing on how they cope with pressure that they will invariably have to face.

If we were to constantly remember Sadhu Gnanmunidas's words and learn to feed off pressure like Dr Carson, we could handle pressure better ourselves and also teach our children by example.

Courage is grace under pressure.

— Ernest Hemingway

Making Mistakes, Acce_

The greatest mistake you can make in life is to be continually fearing you will make one.

— Elbert Hubbard

When we teach our children how to ride a bicycle, we know they will fall. Only when they fall will they learn to ride. While in some instances we are liberal and allow or even encourage mistakes, in most instances, we tend to be overprotective or judgemental. We worry about children making mistakes about the choice of subjects in school and college, choosing the wrong profession or, most importantly, deciding on a life partner. When children tell their parents about their mistakes, they often get scolded. As children grow older, they stop sharing their mistakes, as the earlier experience conditions their minds not to share, but to hold within. It is, therefore, crucial that we form a relationship with our children at a young age that not only allows them the freedom to make mistakes but also gives confidence to talk about where and when they have faltered. In this case, imbibing Mahatma Gandhi's words, 'Freedom is not worth having if it does not include the freedom to make mistakes,' would be ideal.

When one of Devaang's sporting heroes, Tiger Woods, made the headlines, not for winning, but because of his inappropriate behaviour, I saw that Devaang was dejected. So I told him, 'We make mistakes, we all do, even Tiger Woods. That is what makes us human. What is important is to learn from each mistake so that it is never repeated.'

History is full of examples of how mistakes have altered the course of events. Retelling them in the light of their positive outcomes can give children the confidence that mistakes need not be associated only with negativity.

The best example of this is Emperor Ashoka. When Ashoka saw soldiers in pain, wailing wives and orphaned children after he had conquered Kalinga, he was filled with overwhelming remorse. He underwent a transformation and decided to observe dhamma (path of righteousness) and teach others about it as well. He spread the message of ahimsa across his empire and played a major role in spreading Buddhism even beyond his empire. More than 2,000 years have passed since Ashoka's reign ended, but he is still remembered as an ideal ruler.

Another such example is Mahatma Gandhi. Gandhi committed a theft when he was fifteen. He stole a bit of gold out of his brother's armlet but couldn't bear the guilt and made up his mind to confess to his father. While he did not want to hurt his father's feelings, he knew that a confession was required.

He wrote in his autobiography, *The Story of My Experiments with Truth*,

> I wrote it on a slip of paper and handed it to him myself. In this note not only did I confess my guilt, but I asked adequate punishment for it, and closed with a request to him not to punish himself for my offence . . . He read it through, and pearl-drops trickled down his cheeks, wetting the paper. For a moment he closed his eyes in thought and then tore up the note . . . I had thought that he would be angry, say hard things . . . [b]ut he was so wonderfully peaceful. (Gandhi, 1927)

Without hurdles, there is no learning. It is not just ordinary men and women who make mistakes. Those destined to become great do so too.

Thomas Alva Edison had 1,093 inventions to his credit. When he invented a light bulb, a journalist asked him, 'Mr Edison, how did it feel to fail 999 times?' Edison replied, 'I have not failed 999 times. I have simply found 999 ways how not to create a light bulb' (Chinsky, 2012). Each time he did not succeed, he learnt from that mistake. His resolve grew stronger with each mistake and he finally invented the light bulb, exemplifying the fact that there are no mistakes in life, only lessons.

Thomas Watson, the founder of IBM, once said, 'The way to succeed is to double your error rate.' In the 1940s, a mistake by an IBM employee cost the company a whopping one million dollars. Fearing termination, the employee handed over his resignation to Watson, only to be told, 'Fire you? I've just invested one million dollars in your education, and you think I'm going to fire you?'

When children get criticized by family, friends and teachers, even ridiculed for the mistakes they make, they need reassurance—reassurance of the kind that only parents can provide. Unfortunately, quite often, they get the opposite of that. When they get judged, and judged often, the bridge they want to walk on gets burnt. It is not that parents should not discuss mistakes with children. They should, but with an open mind in a non-judgemental manner, focusing more on the future rather than on the past. More time should be spent discussing how to prevent the same mistake again rather than criticizing the past. John Maxwell put it beautifully, 'A person must be big enough to admit his mistakes, smart enough to profit from them and strong enough to correct them.' If our children see us correct our mistakes, they will develop the confidence to confess to us about their own mistakes in the hope that we will help correct them.

We want our children to be flawless. We believe that their flaws will jeopardize their future. In our quest for correcting their flaws, we often damage our relationships. Our children need to know that we have confidence in their abilities in spite of their imperfections. One way of conveying this is to talk about people who have achieved success in the presence of obvious flaws, by making sure that their other qualities shine through.

Winston Churchill was the architect of Britain's victory in World War II. While he was considered a brilliant and charismatic leader, critics thought he was stubborn and arrogant. Churchill also made several mistakes in his career.

He changed parties twice. He was instrumental in sending troops to Turkey in World War I, which resulted in the loss of numerous lives and precious resources. While he made errors of judgement, Churchill had the wisdom to recognize them and change course. He displayed extraordinary leadership in very difficult circumstances to boost the morale of his nation. Under him, the British people believed that they could win the war. He gave people hope and finally victory. His flaws and mistakes did not prevent him from becoming one of the finest leaders Britain has seen.

Even folklore has many such examples to offer. I particularly like to tell parents the story about the two pots.

There was once a water bearer who travelled a long distance to bring water from a stream to his master's home. He carried two pots, one at each end of a long pole. While one pot was perfect, the other pot had a crack. The perfect pot was able to deliver water to its full capacity, while the pot with the crack was able to deliver only half of its capacity. The cracked pot was really sad and said to the water bearer, 'I am so sorry. I am a liability. Half the water you put in me is lost because of my crack. You work hard, yet because of my flaw, you are unable to take two full pots of water to your master. You should discard me and get another perfect pot.' The water bearer smiled and replied, 'When we go back home tomorrow, please watch the path.' The next day the cracked pot noticed beautiful flowers along the road. When they reached home, the cracked pot said, 'While I enjoyed looking at the beautiful flowers, I felt so inadequate.' The water bearer replied, 'There are flowers only on your side. I knew that water would leak from you as we walked home. I, therefore, planted flower seeds on your side of the path. It is because of you that I have been able to take flowers to my master. It is your flaw that has added to the beauty of my master's home.'

Just like the two pots, our children might not be equally accomplished. Despite similar upbringing and education, one child might turn out to be a little less accomplished. Yet, each child makes his or her own precious contribution to the family in his or her own unique way. As parents, we need to love our children equally and accept their shortcomings. In fact, we should find goodness in their imperfections just like the water bearer. Some children are vivacious, others are quiet. Some excel in academics, others in sports. Some like to be left alone, others prefer hand-holding. It is not for us to decide who is better, who is exceptional and who is perfect. Our role as parents is to give love unconditionally.

We as parents also sometimes do not realize that when we complain about the flaws in our children, we are not perfect ourselves. Mahatma Gandhi once said, 'I look only to the good qualities of men. Not being faultless myself, I won't presume to probe into the faults of others.' We need to accept the fact that we aren't perfect and neither are our children.

Man will ever remain imperfect, and it will always be his part to try to be perfect.

— M.K. Gandhi

Be a Dreamer

*The future belongs to those who believe in the beauty of
their dreams.*

— Eleanor Roosevelt

Nandini and I were so excited when we were invited to the
United States Services Club in Delhi to witness a historic
event on a giant screen. Barack Obama was to be sworn in
as the forty-fourth president of the United States. 'A dream
come true, not just for millions of Americans, but also millions
across the globe,' Nandini said in excitement. History was
created in the moment that Barack Obama took the oath with
his hand placed on the Bibles used by Abraham Lincoln and
Dr Martin Luther King Jr. The next day, Devaang asked us
about the inauguration. I told him that Abraham Lincoln and
Dr Martin Luther King Jr had dreamt about this. 'Dad, what
did the inauguration have to do with Abraham Lincoln and
Dr Martin Luther King Jr?' I took this as an opportunity to
tell our son how they had laid the foundation for this dream.

There perhaps could not have been a better opportunity to share the power of a dream—a dream that connected Abraham Lincoln, Dr Martin Luther King Jr and Barack Obama—a dream so powerful that it changed the lives of millions of people.

Abraham Lincoln was born in a log cabin with dirt floors. While growing up in the frontier, he received less than twelve months of formal school education, but he was determined to become a legislator. Three years after his first unsuccessful attempt, he became a legislator, serving for four terms. He then set his sights on becoming a senator. This time, his first and second attempts were unsuccessful. However, he became a national figure with his spirited campaign and famous speech in which he said, 'A house divided against itself cannot stand. I believe this government cannot endure, permanently, half slave and half free. I do not expect the Union to be dissolved, I do not expect the house to fall, but I do expect it will cease to be divided' (Lincoln, 1858).

Lincoln did not give up. He had a dream, and nothing was going to stop him. In 1861, he was elected as the sixteenth president of the United States. Faced with major challenges, he displayed exemplary statesmanship and kept the Union together. In January 1863, he issued the Emancipation Proclamation, which freed 3 million of the 4 million slaves and paved the way for the emancipation of all slaves.

By July 1865, only months after Lincoln's assassination, nearly all 4 million slaves had become free. The Thirteenth Amendment was adopted on 6 December 1865 and declared, 'Neither slavery nor involuntary servitude, except as a punishment for crime whereof the party shall have been duly convicted, shall exist within the United States or any place subject to their jurisdiction' (The Thirteenth Amendment, 1865).

110 years after Lincoln's birth, Dr Martin Luther King Jr was born into a family of pastors. King completed his doctorate from Boston University and became a pastor in Montgomery, Alabama. When Rosa Parks was arrested for refusing to give up her bus seat to a white man, King spearheaded the Civil Rights Movement. He began organizing protests by African Americans and fearlessly led the peaceful protests, even as the white population resisted desegregation and resorted to violence. Despite extreme provocation, King adhered to the principles of non-violence under the strong influence of Mahatma Gandhi's successful non-violent campaign against the British Empire. His house was bombed, he was assaulted four times, arrested more than twenty times and suffered racial abuse on numerous occasions, but he soldiered on, undeterred. King's leadership brought the Civil Rights Movement to the centre stage in American politics.

In 1963, King led more than 250,000 supporters to Washington, DC. Through his powerful speech, King created what many regard as the defining movement in the Civil Rights Movement. He deviated from the written text when Mahalia Jackson shouted, 'Tell them about the dream, Martin!' and said, 'I have a dream that my four little children will one day live in a nation where they will not be judged by the colour of their skin, but by the content of their character. I have a dream today' (King, 1964). The Civil Rights Act was signed into law in 1964. As the leader of the Civil Rights Movement, King travelled more than

6 million miles, delivered more than 2,500 speeches and wrote five books.

What if Abraham Lincoln and Dr Martin Luther King Jr had not had a dream? The world would not have seen such fine leaders, and slavery in the US may not have been abolished when it was. The world as we know it today would have been different.

A hundred years after Lincoln took the presidential oath, Barack Obama was born in Hawaii. After graduating from Harvard Law School magna cum laude, he started practising as a civil rights lawyer. He served for a while as Illinois state senator, and in 2004, became a US senator. On 4 November 2008, Barack Obama made history by winning the presidential election. A colleague of Dr King's, Rev. Joseph Lowery, said in an interview on the occasion of the inauguration that Obama 'epitomizes what Martin Luther King stood for' (Sullivan, 2013). Beverly Robertson, president of the National Civil Rights Museum in Memphis, commented, 'Dr King talked about his dream, but Barack represents the manifestation of that dream.'

Facing the Lincoln Memorial, Barack Obama took the oath of office for the second time in 2013, on Dr Martin Luther King Jr Day, the year that marked 150 years of the Emancipation Proclamation and fifty years of Dr King's March on Washington. What was symbolic was that he placed his hand on two Bibles—one owned by Abraham Lincoln and the other by Dr Martin Luther King Jr, his two heroes (Associated Press, 2013).

'Lincoln, King and Obama had the courage to visualize a dream that most people believed would never turn into reality. It did. No dream is too big. Try to remember that,' I told Devaang as our discussion drew to a close.

Unlike many adults, children like to dream. When adults see their dreams unfulfilled, they lose enthusiasm. Children are different. I often see parents, teachers and relatives inadvertently crushing dreams by telling their children their ideas are not feasible or warning them to be cautious and practical. I like to recount Monty Roberts's story to them when I witness such instances.

Monty Roberts grew up moving from one farm to another as his father was a horse trainer. In senior school, he was asked to write a paper on what he would like to do in life. He wrote about his dream to own a horse ranch and included a drawing of a 4,000-sq.-ft house in the middle of a 200-acre ranch. When he received the graded paper, he was shocked to see an F. The teacher asked Monty to see him after class. The teacher explained that his goal was unrealistic, given the financial status of his family, and suggested that Roberts resubmit his paper. Roberts told the teacher, 'You can keep your F, and I will keep my dream.'

Years later, the teacher took thirty kids to spend a week at a horse ranch. The ranch belonged to Roberts, and he had hung his framed school paper over the fireplace. As the teacher was leaving the ranch, he went over to Roberts and told him that he had been a dream stealer. He was happy that Roberts had not given up on his dream (Miller, 2011).

At the Delhi launch of his autobiography, *Playing It My Way*, Sachin Tendulkar spoke about the importance of dreams. He said, 'Dreams are really important. Many times we work hard and stop short of the last bit of effort we need to realize our dream. . . . When I saw India lift the World Cup in 1983, my dream to win the World Cup was born. It took twenty-eight years to see my dream come true. Every child should have a dream.'

Often, when I interact with families in my clinic, parents make comments such as:

'My child is a dreamer. She doesn't understand that to be successful, you have to plan and study hard. Dreams cannot take you far.'
'Dreams, dreams and dreams; that's all I can get from my son.'
'My daughter doesn't understand the harsh realities of life. Life is not about dreams.'

In India, parents tend to drive home the importance of success in discussions with children at a rather young age. All of us would agree that dreams alone cannot guarantee success. However, everyone needs a dream: a dream to motivate, a dream to excite, a dream to visualize success, a dream to experience the thrill of achievement and a dream to live by.

We should ask our children about their dreams. We should take them to see monuments that stand testament to someone's dream becoming a reality. The Eiffel Tower, the Empire State Building, the Sydney Opera House, the Taj Mahal, among many others, stand today because someone dreamt about them. Every invention was born out of a dream—the light bulb, the DVD, the computer, the cell phone—the list is endless. We need to tell our children that the inventions they are so dependent on are the result of someone's dream. Every museum has examples of dreams coming true. When children see what dreams can achieve, they start believing in theirs. Belief, as we know, is power. The next time our children talk about their dreams, we should let them. In fact, we should encourage them. Their dreams might just change the world.

Every great dream begins with a dreamer. Always remember, you have within you the strength, the patience, and the passion to reach for the stars to change the world.

— Harriet Tubman

Find Your Calling

Your work is going to fill a large part of your life, and the only way to be truly satisfied is to do what you believe is great work. And the only way to do great work is to love what you do. If you haven't found it yet, keep looking. Don't settle. As with all matters of the heart, you'll know when you find it.

— Steve Jobs

Children are often advised on what profession to choose. In India, this advice is offered by parents as early as middle school. Quite frequently, at the end of a consultation, parents of a child in sixth or seventh grade will say something like, 'Doctor, please tell our son that he must make up his mind on what he wants to do when he grows up. It is already too late. So many other children in his class have chosen their profession. You too must have chosen your career by the time you were our child's age.' Backed into a corner by the parent and with opposite views, I usually say, 'There are so many career options today, and it takes time to decide what one really enjoys. I am sure he will decide soon enough.'

In the ninth standard, children are often sent off to coaching classes after a gruelling day at school to prepare for entrance exams for a coveted engineering college, medical college or law school. For four years, these teenagers toil to make it to the merit list. Only a minuscule proportion of them succeed. Thousands are disappointed. Many decide to work even harder for another year to improve their scores. Some, I suspect, are relieved at not finding their name in the list of selected candidates as they perhaps never wanted to do medicine, engineering or law in the first place. They went through years of coaching classes because they could not tell their parents that they wanted to follow their hearts and choose a different profession. Many just did not have the courage to tell their parents that they simply had not decided. They just went down the path of least resistance. After all, who says you have to decide at fourteen, sixteen or eighteen?

What about all those who got into a top professional college? Were they really interested in the course they were pursuing? I have friends who are exceptionally intelligent and had made it to the merit list of both a top medical college and a good engineering college. They chose medicine because it is regarded as one of the most honourable professions in India or because one or both parents were doctors. Two decades later, when I meet them and see the glow in their eyes when we talk about new technology, I can sense their regret of having gone to a medical college instead of an engineering one. They are extremely successful as doctors, but what if they had become engineers? They may have spearheaded inventions that could have had a huge impact. But that did not happen, only because they chose a profession that was not their calling. Many times, following your heart is really hard and hampered by several challenges, such as family pressure, financial circumstances, fear of failure, hesitation to move beyond a comfort zone or even the age factor. Some people cannot even contemplate change because they are older.

Albert Schweitzer, however, was an outlier. Born into a family of pastors, teachers and musicians in France, Albert showed an interest in music at the age of five. He learnt to play the piano, but the organ fascinated him more. He began to play the church organ when he was just eight. At the age of eighteen, he joined a university to study theology, philosophy and music. He excelled in college and completed a doctorate in theology. He became a pastor and wrote two books—*Mystery of the Kingdom of God* and *J.S. Bach: Le Musicien-Poète*, a study of the life of Johann Sebastian Bach—which made him famous. He started receiving several invitations as a speaker and organist.

At the age of thirty, Schweitzer stunned his family and friends by announcing that he was going to join a medical school. He decided to devote his life to serving the people of French Equatorial Africa. 'I wanted to be a doctor so that I might be able to work without having to talk. For years, I had been giving myself out in words,' he said (Kerr, 1994). At the age of thirty-eight, after training for seven years to become a doctor, he set sail for Africa with his wife, Helene, who was a nurse. In a jungle a few miles from the equator, he set up a small health facility in Lambarene (now Gabon). The compound was designed as a simple facility that cared for the needy and the sick, run with the motto that 'simple people need simple healing methods'. The climate was hostile, resources extremely limited and the need immense. The spectrum of diseases encountered was vast. Within a few months of his arrival, he had seen 2,000 patients.

Schweitzer and Helene were taken prisoner during World War I. After being released from prison, Albert raised money for the hospital by giving organ recitals in Europe. Volunteers, nurses and other physicians joined the facility to offer their services. As word spread about the excellent care at the hospital, patients travelled for hours for treatment, which was believed to be the best in the country.

Schweitzer made a huge difference in the lives of the people he served. He was the only hope for many people. His work drew global attention and inspired many to follow suit. Over the years, the Albert Schweitzer Hospital expanded substantially and had seventy buildings, 350 beds and a leper village. The hospital treated almost 30,000 patients each year.

Schweitzer was honoured with numerous degrees, citations, stamps, medals (the British Order of Merit) and the Nobel Peace Prize. Not one who was impressed with recognition, he took two years to accept the Nobel Peace Prize in person.

His resolve to help others at the age of ninety was as strong as it was at thirty. 'You must give some time to your fellow men. Even if it's a little thing, do something for which you get no pay but the privilege of doing it,' he once said (Marshall and Polig, 1971).

Schweitzer was a musician, writer and lecturer. He was a theologian, philosopher and thinker. He was a builder, architect and administrator. He was a mentor, guide and leader. He was a pharmacist, a psychologist and, above all, a good doctor. He had the conviction to find his calling and the courage to devote his life to his calling against many challenges, including going to medical school at the age of thirty, which would hold back most men.

If thirty is a daunting age, imagine breaking away from a settled career at almost seventy. At the age of sixty-nine, A.C. Bhaktivedanta Swami Prabhupada decided to establish the International Society for Krishna Consciousness (ISKCON) in the US. Over the next ten years, he travelled across the globe as many as twelve times and established ISKCON centres across the world and the world's largest vegetarian food relief programme.

We have always been taught that success requires a fine education, but the achievements of many people who chose an unconventional path negate this idea. Soichiro Honda, the founder of Honda Motor Company, once famously said, 'A diploma is less useful than a ticket to a movie' (www.motorcyclemuseum.org, 2000). Honda was speaking from personal experience.

Honda was born in a small village, where his father worked as a blacksmith who also repaired bicycles. While Honda enjoyed helping his father, he did not enjoy school work. Once, to save his family the embarrassment of having to stamp a poor school report card, he devised a stamp using a rubber bicycle pedal cover. He also made forged stamps for other children, for which he was caught and reprimanded.

When he was very young, a car drove through his village. He ran behind the car and stuck his hand in the oil puddle left by the car. Many years later, Honda recounted, 'I could never forget the smell of oil it gave off (Honda Worldwide, 1936). That day, a little boy discovered his calling: Soichiro Honda wanted to make automobiles.

At the age of fifteen, he joined an automobile workshop in Tokyo as an apprentice. For six years, he worked as a mechanic and learnt all there was to learn about engines. He then moved to Hamamatsu and set up a garage, which became popular. In his heart, however, he wanted to build automobiles. His first entry into manufacturing was to start making metal pistons. The project was not initially successful, so he decided to study metallurgy by enrolling in a technological institute. He completed his studies, but dropped out of college because he refused to take the examination. He believed engineering was not just applied science; it was imagination made real and useful. After many experiments, he created perfect piston rings. But, what he really wanted was to create cars. After World War II, when Japan's economy plummeted, Honda went back to repairing cars. He disliked travelling to work by train and as riding a bicycle was slow, he created a mini, low-cost motorcycle. A local businessman, Takeo Fujisama, became interested in this motorcycle and decided to help Honda. The Honda Motor Company was thus born. It became the world's largest manufacturer of motorcycles, producing one million units per month. Honda, however, was not satisfied because his dream remained unchanged.

He approached the Ministry of International Trade and Industry with a proposal for making cars, and was told that he should continue to manufacture motorcycles as only a handful of automakers were part of the Ministry's plan for auto-making. Honda, however, did not take no for an answer. He stunned Japanese and US automakers by focusing on the US market. Honda became the first Japanese auto company to manufacture cars in the US. Toyota and Nissan followed. Honda Motor Company became the world's largest manufacturer of internal combustible engines by volume and Japan's second-largest automaker.

Honda was honoured with Japan's highest honour, the Blue Ribbon. He received honorary doctorates from Michigan Technical University and Ohio State University. He had 470 inventions and 150 patents to his name, even though he did not have a university diploma. For parents whose children are not interested in academics, Soichiro Honda's life is a source of great strength. Especially in India, we tend to focus more than necessary on academics.

Nandini and I did not want Devaang to go through what some of our friends' children had to endure. When he was sixteen, we suggested that he should see a career counsellor and take a psychometric test. The purpose of the counselling and test was to help identify a career path that really interested him because with more than 3,000 career options, it can be a mind-boggling task.

We often do not ask our children what they love doing. We ask them about professions, not passions. We don't seek to recreate what Thomas Edison felt when he said, 'I never did a day's work in my life; it was all fun.' We give our children examples of relatives who have become successful and push them to emulate these people. We forget that children dislike being compared to others. Statements like 'You should become a doctor like your cousin' or 'You could be like your older brother and become an engineer' rub children the wrong way and often make them want to do exactly the opposite.

Instead of relatives, we should talk to children about their role models. All children like that. When we have a conversation about their role models, we can drive home the point that 'If you want to be as successful as Shaquille O'Neal, Cristiano Ronaldo, Jeff Immelt, Amartya Sen or anyone else, you need to find your calling.' We need to make children realize that their heroes achieved what they did because for them their profession was their passion, and work was pure joy.

Parents will be surprised when they have an open discussion with their children about what they really want to do. Parents, in fact, need to be prepared to hear choices that seem scary. Anyway, isn't receiving shocks part of the job description of a parent?

In my clinic, I have a few photographs of celebrities who have over the years supported my work on creating awareness about diseases. A few years ago, a thirteen-year-old girl, Ilishaa, stopped next to a photo of an actress and said, 'You know, Dr Sibal, one day when I become a superstar, you will put up my photo in your clinic.' Divya, her mother, was surprised. 'I was going to tell you in a couple of years that my dream is to be a superstar,' the young lady explained. Now, whenever Ilishaa comes over for a consultation, she talks about her dream. Ilishaa is lucky. Her parents are supportive. They will let her find her calling. Many parents do not.

Albert Schweitzer, A.C. Bhaktivedanta Swami Prabhupada and Soichiro Honda achieved what they did because of one reason. They found their calling. We too must help our children and set them on their path to their calling.

Everyone can rise above their circumstances and achieve success if they are dedicated to and passionate about what they do.

— Nelson Mandela

Compassion

*If you want others to be happy, practice compassion. If you
want to be happy, practice compassion.*

— His Holiness the Fourteenth Dalai Lama

When we were growing up, we were taught to be kind, caring
and compassionate. Some of us remembered what we were
told and imbibed these values at least partially in our lives. In
a few remarkable individuals, however, compassion is evident
in their actions every day.

In November 2006, I had just returned from Kolkata, where
Mother Teresa had established the Missionaries of Charity. Early
on, Devaang and I had made it a ritual to have a conversation
after every trip about the city I had visited. This time, I wanted to
tell him about Mother Teresa's work. However, we did not get
a chance to chat as that evening we went to watch *The Queen*, a
movie based on the events following Princess Diana's tragic death.

The following day, a lazy Sunday, we started talking
about Mother Teresa and Princess Diana.

Here were lives of two ladies who could not have been more different in terms of their upbringing, social circumstances and the nature of their work. They were so different, yet bound by the common quality of compassion.

Mother Teresa was born in Albania. At the age of twelve, she decided that she would become a nun. She left home when she was eighteen to join the Sisters of Loreto and was selected to work in India soon after. She started out by teaching at a school in Darjeeling.

During her time as a teacher, Mother Teresa was disturbed to see the suffering and poverty outside the convent walls. When she was travelling from Calcutta (now Kolkata) to Darjeeling, she experienced what she described as 'the call within the call'. Two years later, she received permission to begin her work with the poor. She gave up the Loreto robes and started wearing a white cotton sari with a blue border. In 1950, she received permission from the Vatican to set up the Missionaries of Charity. The mission in Mother Teresa's words was 'To care for the hungry, the naked, the homeless, the crippled, the blind, the lepers, all those people who feel unwanted, unloved, uncared for throughout society, people that have become a burden to the society and are shunned by everyone' (Johnson, 2011).

Lady Diana was born into the aristocratic Spencer family. When she was nineteen, she was engaged to Prince Charles, the first in line to the British throne. When Diana married Charles at the age of twenty at St Paul's Cathedral, the marriage was a global event. Never before had any royal occasion generated such euphoria. Never before had 750 million people witnessed a single event on television. Diana became 'Her Royal Highness, Princess of Wales'.

While Princess Diana found it difficult to cope with the pressure of her status, she was drawn to doing charitable work. She became the patroness of several organizations that worked for the upliftment of drug addicts, the homeless and the elderly. She learnt sign language as part of her commitment to the British Deaf Association, supported the Royal Marsden Hospital and became the president of Great Ormond Street Hospital for sick children and Barnardo's (a charity for vulnerable children and young people). She displayed limitless energy to propagate her charitable work. At one point in time, she was involved with more than 100 charities.

What drew worldwide attention was her interest in activities that were radically different from what the British Royal Family had traditionally been involved in. This included her work with those afflicted by leprosy and AIDS.

Princess Diana touched those who no one was willing to touch. She talked about those who no one wanted to remember. In every interaction associated with her charitable work, her compassion was evident. Diana contributed to abolishing the stigma that AIDS spreads by touch and became one of the earliest celebrities worldwide to hold and hug AIDS patients. Through her work at the National AIDS Trust, she visited Africa many times, and through the publicity she generated, revolutionized the discourse on AIDS.

After her divorce, Princess Diana became known for supporting the international campaign to ban landmines. She toured Angola and visited a minefield. She spoke about the horrors of landmines in England, the US, Bosnia and Herzegovina.

On the other hand, Mother Teresa had no resources when she set out to work with the poorest of the poor. The initial years were very hard, and she thought of returning to the convent. However, volunteers soon began to join her, and financial support slowly started trickling in. She established hospices, orphanages and homes for leprosy, AIDS and tuberculosis patients, soup kitchens, dispensaries, clinics and schools. Her work spread beyond Calcutta. She established centres in other parts of India, eventually setting up 610 foundations in 123 countries.

When Mother Teresa was awarded the Nobel Peace Prize, she requested that the dinner be cancelled. She felt that USD 7,000 would be better spent feeding 400 people in Calcutta for a year.

Mother Teresa and Princess Diana met once in New York at the Convent of the Missionaries of Charity in June of 1997. Mother Teresa embraced Diana and walked with her arm in arm. They talked about compassion. They talked about the need to do so much and their beliefs. However, that was their first and last meeting. Diana died in a tragic car accident on 31 August 1997 and Mother Teresa passed away a week later on 5 September 1997. Two leading lights of compassion were taken away from the world within seven days.

Does compassion require a superhuman effort? No. Each of us is capable of compassion. Often, we underestimate the power of small acts. A kind word, a kind action, a kind gesture or a kind letter can make a big difference to someone's life.

Children demonstrate compassion in their own simple manner, far removed from the complexities that adults display. For the acts of compassion, they expect no recognition or reward. Children by nature are compassionate. Adults can, in fact, unknowingly discourage that compassion by trying to control how their children interact with other children, adults and animals. A child may want to feed a stray dog but a parent, out of concern for the child's safety and hygiene, might stop him. A child might want to part with the most expensive toy he or she has, but a parent might say, 'Don't give away that toy; it is too expensive. Give a chocolate instead.' Children do not understand the materialistic ways of the world that are an integral part of adult life.

The parents of a seven-year-old girl brought her to me for a consultation as they were concerned about her growth. She had not been gaining adequate weight over the last six months. Her parents felt that she ate well at home and seemed to have no medical problems. The girl studied in a school that was really far from her home. Her home was the first stop for the school bus in the morning and the last stop on the way back. This meant that she had to leave home at 6:45 a.m. and returned at 4:00 p.m. She only had a glass of milk in the morning before she left. In addition to lunch, her mother packed her two snacks, one for the morning and one for the afternoon. Her snack box and lunch box came back empty. As I calculated her dietary intake, I felt that she was being provided with adequate calories. I asked her if she liked what was provided to her, and she said yes. I asked her if she threw away her food sometimes (children often do) and she said no. She did not seem to have any symptoms and the examination was entirely normal. I was really at a loss. I felt there was no need for any investigations as the child appeared to be in good health. I suggested to the family that we should meet again in a month.

When I saw the girl again, she had not gained any weight at all. She had no symptoms, and again the examination was normal. The mother reiterated that the snack box and lunch box came home empty and the girl had no complaints about the food she was provided. In the first consultation, she had been asked about throwing away her food. This time I asked her, 'Do you finish your snacks and meal?' She replied, 'Doctor, my friend and I do.' When I asked her to elaborate, she said, 'My friend does not like the snacks and lunch she gets. Her mother died several months ago, and the nanny gives her the same snacks and lunch every day. If she takes the snacks and lunch back, she is scolded. As I also don't like her food, we throw it away, and she and I eat what I take to school.' Her mother hugged her and started to cry. Her father asked her, 'Why did you not tell us? We could have packed two snack and lunch boxes for you and your friend.' The girl just smiled and said, 'I did not want to trouble Mummy.' The girl had not thought twice about giving away half her food every day. She did not think about herself. For her, friendship stood above everything else.

A friend told me a touching story not so long ago. An eight-year-old girl was struggling to finish her meal. Her anxious mother nudged her husband to explain to their daughter the importance of finishing her meal. 'Go tell her that she needs to eat well to grow. She needs to realize that she must be healthy. You must tell her because she only listens to you.' The father went to the dining table and said, 'Darling, please eat. Eat for your sake. Eat for your mom's sake. Eat for my sake.' The girl said, 'I will, Daddy, even though I don't want to eat this. But first promise me one thing. Will you give me what I want if I finish the meal?' Without hesitating, the father said, 'Fine, I promise.' The daughter then asked, 'This is a promise from mummy as well?' Now the father started to get worried and asked, 'You are not going to ask for something expensive, are you?' 'Not at all, Daddy,' she said reassuringly. After the little girl finished the meal, she went up to her father and gently said, 'Daddy, I want to have my head shaved.' The father did not know how to react. The mother was aghast and shouted, 'No way!' Her father tried to reason with her, 'How about something else? Please reconsider.' But the girl was determined. 'I ate what I detest and now that I have done what I had agreed to do, please do not go back on your word. I have always been taught by both of you that a promise is a promise.' The parents realized that if they went back on their word, their daughter would lose faith in all they had taught her. The girl was taken to the salon over the weekend, and her head was shaved.

The next morning, the father dropped the little girl to school. As she entered the school gate with her clean-shaven head, she waved to her father. Just then a boy called out and asked her to wait for him. The boy too had a clean-shaven head. Pressing the ignition, the father thought to himself, 'This must be some weird new fashion trend.' As he was about to drive away, a lady came up to him and said, 'My son and your daughter are in the same class. My son was diagnosed with blood cancer a few months ago. As a result of chemotherapy, he lost all his hair. He was anxious about rejoining school because he knew he would get teased. Your daughter told him not to worry about teasing. She was going to take care of it. Little did I realize that an eight-year-old would make such a big sacrifice of shaving off her beautiful long hair. You are so lucky to have such a compassionate daughter. She is an amazing human being.' The father was astonished! When he reached home, he told his wife what the lady had said. They realized that they were blessed to have such a caring and compassionate daughter. An eight-year-old had demonstrated compassion in a manner they would never forget.

We could do our children a big favour by not interfering with their acts of compassion. We could go a step further and encourage them when we see them do their best to be kind and thoughtful. In fact, we could learn from our children.

Compassion brings us to a stop, and for a moment we rise above ourselves.

— Mason Cooley

Making Others Happy

*Spread love everywhere you go. Let no one ever come to you
without leaving happier.*

— Mother Teresa

A toddler usually laughs 300 times a day—an adult fifteen
times. A toddler is happy to see his or her parents, a toy or
food. Little things give joy to a toddler. As we grow older,
little things stop carrying as much meaning, and the list of
things that bring joy shrinks. What is most worrying is that
these days even children laugh less than they used to a few
decades ago. There is so much stress, anger, frustration and
even hatred that joy has taken a back seat. As parents, we
need to make our children happy. However, as we all know,
that is easier said than done.

If we ask anyone what is on their wish list, happiness will
feature at the top, along with money, good health, love, peace
of mind, fame and longevity. But the question in focus is:
how many of us are happy?

In our quest for happiness, we read, discuss and experiment. We try to change others, our circumstances, jobs—even professions, cities, countries, spouses and friends. We keep trying to make ourselves happy by keeping ourselves at the centre of this quest. Many of those who are happier have tried another approach. Make others happy, and you will find happiness. One person who excelled at this approach was Walt Disney.

Just after turning sixteen, Devaang had returned from a school trip to Disney World and could not stop talking about his trip. He had found his paradise. In keeping with my strategy to instil values by examples rather than lengthy sermons, it seemed natural to talk about the creator of the paradise, Walt Disney.

Every year, more than 100 million people walk into a Disney property with a smile in anticipation of a happy day. They usually have a wonderful time, enjoying the rides and incredible shows. They also get to spend quality time with their family and friends. All these people leave with fond memories and a bigger smile. Millions more smile and laugh when they watch Disney cartoons and films. Perhaps no single man's ideas have made so many people happy over so many generations.

Disney enjoyed drawing from a very young age. His neighbour once asked him to draw a picture of his horse. While the drawing was not great, he received encouragement, inspiring him to draw more energetically. When he was ten, he fell in love with trains. His uncle Michael was an engineer, and Disney would often put his ears to the tracks in anticipation of a train, trying to spot his uncle conducting it.

In high school, he became the cartoonist for the school newspaper and also developed an interest in photography. He attended school during the day, and the Academy of Fine Arts in Chicago at night. When he was turned down by the army and navy during World War II as he was underage, he got a job as a Red Cross ambulance driver. The ambulance he drove in France stood out for its artwork because he had covered it with original sketches.

On his return from France, he got a job as a newspaper artist. He started experimenting with animation and even acquired a studio and called it Laugh-O-Gram. The studio did not do well, and he along with his brother Roy decided to move to California. The brothers hoped that their cartoons would have better luck in the sunny state.

Symbolically, it was on a train that Disney came up with the idea of creating a character based on a mouse. Disney had always been interested in mice, even keeping them in a cage in his studio to keenly observe them. He called this character Mortimer Mouse, but his wife Lillian suggested the name Mickey. While the silent films featuring Mickey were not successful, the first sound film wherein Disney lent his voice for Mickey was a hit. Soon, new friends like Donald Duck, Goofy and Pluto were born.

Disney also took the brave step of creating a full-length animated film called *Snow White and the Seven Dwarfs*. This film's success established the animation film industry. *Pinocchio*, *Bambi*, *Cinderella* and a host of other films followed. What made all Disney productions distinct was that they were created to spread joy.

When he became a father, Disney would take his daughters Diane and Sharon to a merry-go-round in a park. He would wait patiently till the girls were ready to go home.

Diane Disney in an interview with the *San Francisco Chronicle* said, 'As he stood there, he kept thinking there should be more for parents and children to do together, and the idea for Disneyland was born' (*Daily Mail Reporter*, 2013). The idea was to create a place where people could have fun—lots of fun!

Disney himself drew sketches of his ideas for an amusement park. As the plans were being developed, he had said, 'I just want it to look like nothing else in the world. And it should be surrounded by a train' (see the Wikipedia article on 'Walt Disney').

In 1955, thousands of people saw Disney's dream turn into reality when Disneyland was inaugurated in Anaheim, California. In his dedication speech, he said, 'To all who come to this happy place; welcome. Disneyland is your land . . . hope that it will be a source of joy and inspiration to all the world' (Wikipedia, 'Walt Disney'). As Disneyland became incredibly successful, Disney felt the desire to spread the joy beyond the west coast. He decided to establish Disney World in Orlando that would include 'The Magic Kingdom' and the 'Experimental Prototype City' (or community) of Tomorrow (EPCOT).

Walt Disney's work inspired the establishment of amusement parks across the globe, indirectly bringing happiness to countless people on the planet. So profound has been the impact of the culture of the Walt Disney Company that companies far removed from entertainment have studied and adapted their work culture. In his bestseller, *If Disney Ran Your Hospital*, Fred Lee declares that if hospitals could learn from Disney, hospital employees would be driven in their understanding by imagination, imagining what a patient and the patient's family are thinking and experiencing. If hospitals embraced the Disney philosophy, they would become happier places. And if hospitals, where there is so much pain and suffering, can become happier places, one can only imagine that other workplaces could also become places where joy is shared, by following the Disney culture (Lee, 2004).

As parents and adults, we need to ask our children a simple question: 'What makes you happy?' Surprisingly, very few parents I know actually ask their children this question. We tend to assume that a particular activity will do the job. More often than not, when I ask parents what makes their child happy, they have no answer and my question usually draws a blank. Every child is different. Some children like sports; some do not. Some children like being indoors while some like being one with nature. We need to make the effort to find out what would make our child happy. When they see us do what makes them happy, they too would feel the urge to do things that make us happy. When they learn to find happiness by making others happy, they create a ripple effect that spreads happiness to many people.

Charlie Chaplin, one of the biggest stars of the twentieth-century silent film era responsible for bringing many moments of joy and laughter to numerous people, had to go through many hardships as a child. When he was ten, his father died, and his mother developed a serious illness. He spent time in an orphanage. When he was twelve, he acted in a stage show. He then joined the film industry and made a mark with his distinctive style. The pain he had experienced made him focus on humour. He stated, 'To truly laugh, you must be able to take your pain and play with it.' In a famous speech, he said, 'We all want to help one another. Human beings are like that. We want to live by each other's happiness, not by each other's misery' (Chaplin, 1940). Chaplin wrote in his poem 'Smile', 'If you smile through your fear and sorrow/ Smile and maybe tomorrow/ You'll see the sun come shining through/ For you' (Chaplin, 1954). We should remember this and always nudge ourselves and our children to smile, especially when we are feeling low.

I make it a point to call all my patients on their birthdays. Shona Nath, whose three lovely children I look after, told me that it meant a lot to her that I make the effort to call. Ever since, I have tried not to default on this count. No matter which part of the world I am in, I make it a point to make the phone calls. If the child is really young, I wish his/her parents. I cannot accurately describe the sheer happiness I usually sense in the voice on the other end of the phone. Every year, I do my best to make hundreds of families happy, and through them, I too find my dose of joy.

A day without laughter is a day wasted.
— Charlie Chaplin

Never Give Up Hope

*We must accept finite disappointment, but never lose
infinite hope.*

— Dr Martin Luther King Jr

Professor Stephen Hawking was visiting Delhi to deliver a
talk. There was a lot of excitement in Devaang's school about
the visit. As we were watching the news, we began discussing
Professor Hawking's life. Devaang and I spent a couple of
hours on the Web learning about his amazing life.

In 1963, when he was twenty-one, Stephen Hawking
was diagnosed with a serious neurological disease called
amyotrophic lateral sclerosis (ALS) and was told he had only
a few years to live.

ALS is a progressive neurodegenerative disease that affects
neurons. It afflicts 350,000 people a year globally. In ALS,
voluntary muscle actions progressively get affected, day-to-
day activities become difficult, and the individual may be
totally paralysed.

Although Hawking became wheelchair-bound, he went on to Cambridge to become a brilliant researcher at Caius College. From 1979 to 2009, he held the post of Lucasian Professor at Cambridge, the chair held by Isaac Newton in 1663. A Fellow of the Royal Society and a member of the US National Academy of Science, he is regarded as one of the most brilliant theoretical physicists since Einstein.

ALS created many difficulties that Hawking considered challenges that needed to be overcome. Technology, immense will power and hope helped him conquer these challenges. Special computers designed in California allow him to communicate using only two fingers as he has no motor control over his body and is unable to speak any longer. His body has been incapacitated by ALS, but his mind is still working hard trying to unravel the mystery of how the universe was created.

Hawking had once said, 'I'm not afraid of death, but I'm in no hurry to die. I have so much I want to do first.' He is a man who never gave up and never will.

Augusto and Michaela Odone were living in the beautiful Comoros Islands when their five-year-old son, Lorenzo, started to experience behavioural problems. While initially the doctors felt that this might be due to difficulty in adjusting to a foreign environment, Lorenzo's difficulties increased over time. He started to have memory lapses, his eyesight began to fail and he started to have unexplained falls. When he was six, a diagnosis of adrenoleukodystrophy (ALD) was confirmed.

ALD is a rare genetic disorder that is X-linked and hence, primarily occurs in males. It is usually seen in children between the ages of four and ten. The child's condition deteriorates, sometimes rapidly, behavioural problems worsen, coordination becomes impaired, deafness and memory loss are common, swallowing becomes difficult, vision deteriorates and total disability can ensue within a year. This disorder is fatal.

The Odone family consulted the best ALD expert, Dr Hugo Moser, in Baltimore. As there was no specific therapy, Lorenzo joined a clinical trial for a special diet. The diet did not help. Augusto and Michaela Odone were not ready to accept that Lorenzo was going to die. They could have given up. Most parents would have, but they did not.

They started reading about ALD and spent numerous hours at a medical library going through all the published research. They organized the first-ever conference on ALD to bring together all global experts working on the disease. They started to hypothesize on what caused ALD and which therapies might work. In two years, the Odones arrived at a hypothesis that a combination of two cooking oils could inhibit the enzyme that overproduced the very long chain fatty acids. They started administering this oil to Lorenzo through a feeding tube. Lorenzo's fatty acid levels decreased, and Augusto published his findings. On the basis of these findings, Dr Moser felt encouraged to commence all his young ALD patients on this oil.

A family from the UK, the Staffords, flew to the US and started their son, Barry, on the oil. The Staffords discovered that their younger son, Glenn, who was only two and had no symptoms, also had the defective gene. Dr Moser decided to put Glenn on the oil even though he had no symptoms.

Over the years, however, it became clear that Lorenzo's oil could not stop progression in ALD. Barry Stafford and other children died. While Lorenzo remained alive, his condition did not get better. Dr Moser decided not to give up. He started prescribing Lorenzo's oil to boys who had the gene but no symptoms. His trial showed dramatic results. Ten years after starting the boys on Lorenzo's oil, 70 per cent did not develop symptoms. While Lorenzo could not be saved and died at the age of thirty, many lives have been saved since. Glenn Stafford, the first boy with no symptoms to be put on the oil, remains well more than two decades later. Today, the outcomes for ALD are dramatically different. Boys with the defective gene can be identified, and Lorenzo's oil can give them a real chance of not developing the symptoms of this deadly disease. This happened thanks to Augusto Odone, Michaela Odone, Dr Moser and the Stafford family's positive spirit.

As a doctor, I am amazed by the cases that make us reconsider the limits of the human body and the definition of the word 'impossible'. One such case I always marvel at is that of Jody Miller, a happy and mischievous toddler. At the age of three, Jody started having seizures, and was prescribed an antiepileptic medicine. The seizures kept on increasing in frequency and severity, and there were days when she had 100 seizures in twenty-four hours. More antiepileptic medicines were added, but the combination of medicines could not control the seizures. Jody's condition worsened. She developed partial paralysis and could not walk. Jody's parents were told that she suffered from Rasmussen's Encephalitis (RE).

RE is a rare inflammatory brain disease with a terrifying outlook. It occurs in 1 in 500,000–1,000,000 individuals. Affecting only one hemisphere (side) of the brain, RE mostly occurs in previously normal children. It typically affects children between the age of two and ten years. Symptoms are relentless seizures and a rapid decline in cognitive (learning) ability, along with increasing weakness of one side of the body as the disease progresses. The progression takes place over one to two years. Although the precise mechanisms are still uncertain, RE is considered an autoimmune disease. The child's own immune system cells enter the brain, and cause inflammation and damage. The possible trigger could be a viral infection. The inflammation causes permanent brain damage and shrinkage, worsened by the seizures themselves.

Since the seizures continually increase, the only treatment is radical surgery. Radical, perhaps, is describing it mildly. The surgery involves removing half the brain. Yes, half the brain. A radical hemispherectomy is what this procedure is called.

When Jody's parents were told that the only treatment option was a radical hemispherectomy, they were devastated. Any parent would be. Imagine being told as a parent that the only effective treatment is removing half your child's brain— not 10, 20 or 30 per cent, but 50 per cent. What can be more extreme in terms of treatment? We know that each part of the brain controls specific body functions like speech, vision and hearing. Some of these areas that control important functions are as small as a few centimetres. When removing small areas can produce significant effects on normal body functions, what would be the consequences of removing half the brain?

The Miller family understood that as this disease affects only one of the hemispheres, removing that hemisphere would make the seizures go away. But what would happen to all the body functions controlled by that side of the brain? This was the biggest concern that Jody's parents had. Would she be able to use her limbs? Be able to speak, read and write? Go back to school? Back to her happy self before RE afflicted her?

The family chose to go to Dr Ben Carson, the renowned paediatric neurosurgeon who had also visited our hospital to give expert advice. Dr Carson explained the rationale that disconnection of half the brain would make the seizures go away. After the removal of the hemisphere, fluid would fill the empty space that would be created. A child's brain has more neuroplasty, allowing neurons from the remaining hemisphere to take over the tasks from the lost hemisphere. So, in a way, the brain has the ability to rewire itself. Although the arm and hand functions on the opposite side get impaired, children adjust to using the healthy limbs. Even when the language hemisphere is removed, reasonable language skills can be regained. Children do not forget what they had learnt earlier. The younger the child is at the time of surgery, the better is the adaptation. He mentioned that the surgery could take up to twelve hours but rehabilitation could take weeks to months. Dr Carson gave them confidence that Jody would get better.

Jody's family made the most difficult decision and agreed to the surgery, because this was their only hope. The hemispherectomy went off smoothly, but the post-operative period was trying. Jody underwent prolonged rehabilitation and eventually regained her strength. The seizures stopped, and her body learnt to function with half her brain. Slowly but surely, she recovered.

Jody eventually went back to school. At eight, she topped second grade. She completed her university degree. Now, Jody wants to be a teacher. Her mother, Lynn, is now Specialty Director, RE, at the Hemispherectomy Foundation, helping families dealing with RE. There cannot perhaps be a better advocate than Lynn. She knows what it takes to look after a child with RE, the difficulties in dealing with this condition, the strength needed to go ahead with the radical surgery and the patience to see one's child make slow progress post surgery, one step at a time, one function at a time. Above all, she knows how to tell them to never give up hope.

Freya used to have 200 seizures in a day. She underwent hemispherectomy surgery in Melbourne in 2010 and is now seizure-free. Cameron Mott underwent this surgery at the age of nine, and now, six years later, wants to be a ballerina. Seven-year-old Gemma Hockley, a right-hander, had her left hemisphere removed. Four years later, she was playing her favourite sports—soccer and basketball. At school, Gemma was recognized for neat handwriting, an extraordinary achievement considering she now writes left-handed.

Hundreds of children have benefitted from this surgery. Imagine not just functioning but excelling, with only half of your brain. When children with RE, who need to lose half their brain to get better, and their families do not lose hope, how can any of us?

Over the last two decades, Dr Carson has evolved his surgical techniques. While earlier he used to remove the whole hemisphere at once, now he takes it out piecemeal.

This results in less pull on the remaining half of the brain with better outcomes.

We all want to do so much. Quite often, we try and then give up. There are justifiable reasons to give up, or at least reasons that we think are justified. Whenever I hear about people giving up, I tend to tell them about the positive spirit that I see in the families of children with serious illnesses. For them, each day is a struggle. Imagine the trauma of painful tests and injections, the repeated hospitalizations, the side effects of therapy and the risk of opportunistic infections. Despite the uncertainty of the final outcome, families bravely face the challenges. Doctors are so fortunate that each time they feel like giving up, the families of patients they care for inspire them not to. When I find circumstances challenging, all I have to do is to spend extra time with children who are admitted in hospital. My challenges seem trivial in comparison. Teachers and parents need to consider visits to a hospital for a reality check on what are real difficulties in life. A brief interaction can change one's perspective towards challenges that seem insurmountable.

When Devaang talks about difficulties in his life, all I have to do is to remind him about what he has.

There is no medicine like hope, no incentive so great and no tonic as powerful as expectation of something tomorrow.

— Orisen Swett Marden

Determination

Success is not final, failure is not fatal: it is the courage to continue that counts.

— Winston Churchill

In 2010, a newer version of the iPhone was launched. Devaang started making a passionate case for an iPhone, calling it 'so smart' and highlighting that the 'the technology is awesome', 'the touch screen feels so smooth', 'everyone is getting one' and saying, 'Please, please, please can I have one?' Steve Jobs really knew how to get people excited about Apple products. Taking advantage of the excitement that was so palpable in Devaang, I decided to initiate a discussion on Steve Jobs' life. Devaang was surprisingly enthusiastic. I guess Apple had become so much a part of everyday life that he wanted to know about Jobs.

Jobs' life was full of ups and downs, and amazing determination.

Imagine dropping out of college after six months, founding a company at twenty-one, creating a USD 2 billion company with more millionaires than any company in history, being fired from the company he had founded, starting a new company and buying another, being brought back to become the CEO of the company that fired him, or dying at the age of fifty-six after fighting a rare cancer for eight years. Jobs didn't do just any one of those things; he did *all* of them.

After he dropped out of college, Jobs started attending meetings of the Homebrew Computer Club. This group consisted of computer enthusiasts. Here, he met Steve Wozniak, and they decided to work together. Jobs and Wozniak started Apple Computer, Inc. in Jobs' parents' garage in 1976. According to Wozniak, Jobs had suggested the name after visiting a commune on an apple orchard.

Their first creation was the Apple I. This was a computer without a case, keyboard or monitor. In a year, they were ready with the Apple II, which became a huge success. At twenty-five, Steve was worth USD 100 million.

Seven years after setting up Apple Computer, Inc., Jobs reached out to John Sculley at Pepsi-Cola and asked him, 'Do you want to sell sugar water for the rest of your life, or do you want to come with me and change the world?' So, Sculley became the CEO of Apple.

Jobs and Sculley had different management styles, and a power struggle between the two ensued. Low sales made things worse. When the second-generation Mac did not receive a positive response, the conflict between the two reached a breaking point. They disagreed on how to reposition the company, and Sculley went to the board. The board decided to back Sculley, and Jobs was fired.

So what did Jobs do? He became a coffee bean. A coffee bean? you ask. Let me explain.

A young woman whose life was full of troubles went to her mother for advice. Her mother listened patiently as she ranted about her endless challenges and then took her to the kitchen. She filled three pots with water and placed them on the stove. As the water started to boil, she put carrots in one pot, eggs in the second and coffee beans in the third. After a while, she turned off the stove and brought out the three bowls and asked her daughter, 'What do you see in each of the bowls?' 'Carrots, boiled eggs and coffee,' her daughter replied. 'What else?' asked the mother. 'Mom, the carrots are soft, the eggs are hard-boiled and the coffee smells nice. So what's the point you are trying to make?' The mother replied, 'The carrots were stronger before getting into the boiling water, but they came out soft and weak. The eggs went in soft on the inside, with a shell protecting them, but came out hard on the inside. The coffee beans changed the colour and taste of the water. So, what do you want to be?'

So, Jobs, in his coffee-bean mode, started another company. He named it NeXT. Seven years later, he laid off half the employees and closed the factory, and decided to focus on software development. Ten years later, Apple bought the company for USD 400 million.

The year Jobs started NeXT, he bought a computer animation studio named Pixar, turning it around and playing a hand in the successes of *Toy Story*, *Ratatouille*, *The Incredibles* and *Cars*. Ten years after being fired from Apple, he became a billionaire. Next year, he was approached to rejoin Apple.

In his new avatar, Jobs made radical changes at Apple. He fired a large section of managers and dismantled the divisional structure. He hired Tim Cook, who would eventually take over as the CEO. It wasn't just the extent of changes alone he brought about that generated considerable interest in the industry, it was the style as well. While earlier in his career he was often critical of other people's ideas with little patience to even hear their views if they were different, Jobs now had an open mind.

Jobs once commented, 'My model for business is The Beatles. They were four guys that kept each other's negative tendencies in check; they balanced each other. And the total was greater than the sum of the parts. Great things in business are never done by one person; they are done by a team of people' (Jobs and Beahm, 2011). This was very different from how a younger Jobs had worked. The employees were now excited, and they felt a sense of pride in their daily work. The results were a host of innovative products.

In a speech Jobs gave at Stanford University in 2005, he said being fired from Apple was the best thing that could have happened to him: 'The heaviness of being successful was replaced by the lightness of being a beginner again, less sure about everything. It freed me to enter one of the most creative periods of my life.' He added, 'I'm pretty sure none of this [NeXT, Pixar, the iPod and iTunes] would have happened if I hadn't been fired from Apple. It was awful-tasting medicine, but I guess the patient needed it' (Kaul, 2009).

Jobs' philosophy was clear: 'Twenty years from now, you will be more disappointed by the things you didn't do than by the ones you did do. So throw off the bowlines. Sail away from the safe harbour. Catch the trade winds in your sails."

Unlike Jobs, most of us react to failure rather negatively. Frustration, anger and hopelessness are common reactions. The heavens seem to come crushing down when we do not get the promotion we wanted, a project falls apart or we don't get the results we expected to. Our children tend to react in a similar fashion. Failure to make it to the sports team, the choir or the declamation team is seen as a major disappointment. Not becoming a prefect is seen as a calamity.

Devaang thought that he would become the Head Boy of his school. According to his own assessment, his credentials were good, and he deserved the position. When the announcement was made, Devaang was distraught. He was not made the head boy but the deputy head boy. Nandini and I decided to have a chat with him. 'You should be grateful that you were selected to be the deputy head boy. It is quite an honour.' When this did not work, we tried to reason with 'there are fewer responsibilities', 'you have more time to do what you like', 'there is more time to study for your final exams and less pressure'. Nothing seemed to give him solace. However, over the next few days, the disappointment gradually reduced.

Three years later, Devaang expressed a desire to become president of the Commerce Society of his college, Hindu

---

* *This quote has been attributed to Mark Twain, but the attribution cannot be verified. The quote should not be regarded as authentic. See TwainQuotes.com, website edited by Barbara Schmidt, comment at bottom of webpage titled 'Discovery'.*

College. Our advice to him was: 'Do not let the failure in school bother you. Remember Edmund Hillary, who failed at his first attempt of scaling the Everest, but trained harder till he made it. Think of what you can do differently this time.' Devaang became president. When we congratulated him, we told him that he should remember that he might fail the next time he sets his sight on something. Life is about success, failure and more success. The key to facing all of it is the determination to rise after one falls.

The next time our children get disappointed when they taste failure, we need to remind them about determination. An Apple product will usually be in sight to help drive home the point.

Develop success from failures. Discouragement and failure are two of the surest stepping stones to success.

— Dale Carnegie

Giving

When God blesses you financially, don't raise your standard of living. Raise your standard of giving.

— Mark Batterson

The 2009 Forbes list of billionaires had just been released. As we were listening to the news, Devaang commented, 'Every year, it is the same story. Bill Gates is the richest man in the world again; so boring.' 'While he is the richest man on this planet, do you know that he is also the man who has given more to charitable causes than anyone else? Every so often he comes to India to review projects his foundation supports. He is constantly looking out for opportunities to give. Don't you want to learn more about Bill Gates, the man who changed the way we lead our lives?' I asked, hoping that Devaang would say yes.

'I guess I would, considering that if it weren't for him, we wouldn't have Windows.'

And so we embarked on another of our customary father–son research projects and found enough to keep us engaged for a while. Bill Gates left Harvard without completing his course to co-found Microsoft. At the age of thirty-one, he became the youngest self-made billionaire in history. Under his leadership, Microsoft grew into one of the most successful corporations in the world. In 1998, he became the richest man in the world and has consistently held that position every year other than 2010 and 2011. In 2014, his net worth was USD 81.5 billion.

After his mother's untimely death from breast cancer at the age of sixty-four, Gates founded organizations to address causes that were close to his mother. When Gates was getting married, his mother wrote to his bride, Melinda, 'From those to whom much is given, much is expected.' In 2000, Gates, along with Melinda, founded the Bill and Melinda Gates Foundation. The Gates Foundation supports education, agriculture, financial services, information technology and health projects in more than 100 countries and all states of the US. The largest allocation of funds has been to health, notably to the promotion of vaccination. Eradication of polio has become a mission for Gates.

As of 2014, Bill and Melinda had donated USD 30.1 billion. What is remarkable is that over 95 per cent of their wealth has been pledged to their foundation, which will spend all the money within twenty years of their passing.

Gates once said in an interview, 'Money has no utility to me beyond a certain point. Its utility is entirely in building an organization and getting the resources out to the poorest in the world' (Tweedie, 2013). In his famous Harvard Commencement speech in 2007, he had said that the foundation was conceived when he started thinking, 'How can we do the most good for the greatest number with the resources we have?' (Gates, 2007).

Warren Buffet and Bill Gates have been friends since 1991. Buffet has been among the world's four richest men since 2000. In 2006, he made a dramatic announcement that he would give away 85 per cent of his Berkshire Hathaway stock to charity, with the vast majority pledged to the Bill and Melinda Gates Foundation. By 2014, Buffet had gifted more than USD 17 billion to the Gates Foundation. What makes Buffet's generosity extraordinary is that he decided to give his money to a well-established charity rather than create one of the largest philanthropic organizations in the world in his name.

Gates and Buffet together founded 'The Giving Pledge'. Set up in 2009, this campaign encourages the wealthiest of the wealthy across the globe to pledge most of their wealth to philanthropic causes. By 2014, 127 billionaires had signed the pledge, together pledging more than USD 200 billion. Azim Premji, the chairman of Wipro, has pledged USD 2.3 billion and become the largest contributor from India. While the generosity of Bill Gates, Warren Buffet and other billionaires is exemplary, does one need to be rich to be generous? Not at all.

Jorge Munoz is an immigrant from Columbia who lives in New York. By day, he drives a school bus, but in the evening, he has taken on an even more important job: he feeds hungry construction workers in Queens. Munoz gets up at 4:45 a.m. to plan the meal he will serve. After he returns from work, he fills his truck with food that his mother helps prepare, and at 9:30 p.m., distributes food to dozens of labourers. He spends

USD 200 a week, a third of his earnings, on providing these meals. His mission to serve the construction workers each day of the week leaves him no time for friends, hobbies or leisure. When asked what drives him, he said, 'I know these people are waiting for me, and I worry about them. You have to see their smile, man. That's the way I get paid'. If it was not for their guardian angel Munoz, dozens of construction workers would not know where their next meal was coming from (Ellick, 2007).

P. Kalyansundaram, who was recognized as 'the Best Librarian in India' and also 'one of the top ten librarians in the world', led an exemplary life. As a college student, he had wanted to contribute his gold chain when India was at war in 1962. The chief minister had sent him away, urging him to donate something he had earned himself. That incident left a mark on his young mind. For thirty-five years, he donated his entire salary to help the underprivileged. To meet his daily needs, he did odd jobs. 'Paalam', the organization he established, collects donations and distributes them among the needy.

In my own experience as a paediatrician, I have seen numerous heart-warming instances of giving. Nihal Upadhyay was all of nine months when I first saw him. He had been referred to us from Guwahati. He suffered from an inflammatory condition of the liver. Afflicted by jaundice in the first few weeks of life, scarring of the liver (called cirrhosis) had developed. The only treatment for Nihal was a liver transplant.

Nihal's paternal aunt was found to be an appropriate donor. The family was determined to save the child but expressed their inability to raise funds for the transplant. The hospital and the clinical team were happy to perform a free transplant but still needed money for all the medicines and consumables. I decided to request a TV news channel to put in an appeal for donations. The next morning, I received a call from the former cricketer, TV commentator and host, Navjot Singh Sidhu, asking me how much money was needed. I told him, 'Please give us whatever you deem fit.' Navjot sent us a cheque for Rs 18 lakh. Out of that, 6 lakh was used, and the remaining 12 lakh was put into a fixed deposit. The interest on the fixed deposit pays for the anti-rejection medicine that Nihal needs. Navjot did not seek publicity. When I met him to express our gratitude, he said, 'Call me any time you face a similar situation.' Over the years, I have seen so many individuals come forward to help families. Often, these are individuals who have never met these families and may never connect with them as well. Their spirit of giving without seeking any recognition, any praise and any gratitude makes them special. Parul Tuli, Shona Nath and Jasmine Chadha are three such people. Whenever a case for which financial help is required comes in, all I have to do is give them a call and treatment is made possible. All three of them have this desire to help children with limited means who need liver transplants. They belong to a rare breed of people who believe in giving for the sake of giving. Nothing more, nothing less.

Children are usually generous. During the winter holidays, Nandini, Devaang and I wanted to spend a day with Nandini's sister, Priti, and her fourteen-year-old son, Divij. While Nandini, Priti and I were relatively free, Divij was not available as he had a commitment. He and his friends were busy providing a nice meal to underprivileged children.

Over several weeks, Divij and his friends had been collecting money from neighbours and also making generous contributions from their pocket money. They had managed to collect Rs 10,125. When we met him a week later, Divij told us about his experience. The original plan had been to feed 200 children, but because the response was overwhelming, they ended up serving 326 children. As some of the children were too small to eat themselves, they fed the infants with their own hands. I asked Divij, 'How did you come up with this idea?' Divij explained 'Two days before Diwali, Mom and I were going to buy firecrackers. Next to a food stall on the street, I saw two children who seemed hungry. Mom suggested that I should buy food for them. As those two children were eating, more children came up to the stall and lined up for a plate of *chhole kulche*. In one hour, I ended up buying food for sixty-two children. Even though I used up three quarters of the money I had been given for firecrackers, I felt a unique sense of satisfaction. I decided that around Christmas I would organize something bigger. I discussed this with my friends, and we decided to organize this. We will now do this four times a year.' Watching the glow on his face and hearing his enthusiasm, I knew that a fourteen-year-old had discovered the joy of giving.

There is growing evidence that giving is actually beneficial to the giver. Research has shown that acts of kindness result in an increase in serotonin, which is a neurochemical that alleviates depression. Increase in serotonin results in mood elevation and decreases anxiety. In functional MRI scans, regions of the brain that are activated on receiving money show even greater activation when money is given away (Fleming et al., 2010).

Christine Carter, PhD, is a sociologist and happiness expert at UC Berkeley's Greater Good Science Center, whose mission is to teach skills for a thriving, resilient and compassionate society. In an article titled 'What We Get When We Give', she writes that people who volunteer tend to get fewer aches and pains (Carter, 2010). Even just observing someone else engaged in charity was shown to increase the level of immunoglobulin, an important antibody in our immune system (Collins, 2014).

Stephen Post, who co-authored the book *Why Good Things Happen to Good People*, offers sound advice: 'One of the best ways to overcome stress is to do something to help someone else' (Post, 2012).

In an experiment published in *Wellbeing: The Five Essential Elements* by Tom Rath and Jim Harter, individuals were given money to spend. The participants were assigned to spend the money on personal items, buy a gift for someone or give it to charity. The participants who spent the money on a gift or gave to charitable causes experienced a boost in well-being. In contrast, those who spent it on themselves did not (Rath and Harter, 2010).

Most of us are so busy chasing material gratification and amassing wealth that we often forget what Saint Francis of Assisi had said, 'For it is in giving that we receive.' It is not surprising that our children follow us in our pursuit for more. Our children should see us give without expectations, give without recognition and give for the joy of giving. When we do that, they are likely to follow. We could encourage our children to give anything, whether it is a book, a toy or a chocolate, to someone who is not as lucky as them. It could be something small. Something small will, over time, lead to giving something bigger. Once they discover the joy of giving, they will need little encouragement. I have noticed that girls find it easier to share and easier to give. In my clinic, the girls nearly always ask for an extra candy for their brother, but brothers seldom do. Girls will happily share toys or games in the waiting room with other children; boys find it a bit harder. Maybe that is the way nature has programmed boys and girls. Parents of boys, therefore, need to start earlier and work harder to get them to learn to give.

Giving is not only the right thing to do, it is also beneficial for the physical and mental well-being of the giver. We need to remember what Mahatma Gandhi said, 'The fragrance always remains on the hand that gives the rose.' One of the best gifts we can give to our children is to teach them the joy of giving.

Give all, gain all.

— M.K. Gandhi

Be the Change

You must be the change you wish to see in the world.

— M.K. Gandhi

We want to change so much. We want to change borders, policies, the environment, the way business is conducted and the way people behave. We talk about the need for change. We offer solutions on how to bring about change. Most often, in our quest for change, we place the onus to change on someone else. We forget that we actually have little control over the world. What we have control over is ourselves. Yet, we look outside and not within. Mahatma Gandhi's words are so true: 'As human beings, our greatness lies not so much in being able to remake the world—that is the myth of the atomic age—as in being able to remake ourselves.'

We want to change our children. After all, this book is about changing our children—for the better. Our children want to change a lot of things too. Many of us, however, do not know what our children want to change. We do not have that conversation because we do not have the time or we believe that our child is too young to discuss this with. If we have this discussion, we will be surprised at what they say. I sometimes ask children about what they want to alter. They always have lots to say. They don't want homework and exams. They don't want their classmates to tease them. They want the world to be a happier place. For their parents to not be parents all the time. For parents to spend more time with them. They want quality time and individual attention. They want their parents to be role models.

Like us, our children want others to change. They want to see the change but are not willing to change themselves. Ask them if they will stop teasing others and the answer will be, 'But he started it, not me! You want me not to retaliate?'

Among the different values that I have touched upon, the ability to recognize that change has to begin with oneself is the hardest to inculcate. We as parents must first be the change we wish to see in the world and our children. If we do not, we might as well not have this discussion with our children. We hate being criticized, but we criticize our children often. We like to be praised, but how often do we praise our children? We do praise them for winning awards and excelling in academics and sports, but do we praise them for smaller achievements? Do we praise them for good behaviour? We take that for granted, don't we? If we stop criticizing them and become lavish in compliments, they will return the favour.

We often say to ourselves, 'It is so hard to change now; I am so set in my ways.' Then, we should not be surprised to hear from our twelve-year-old, 'I have been doing this for a while; I cannot change now' or 'I would like to change; show me how by changing yourself first.'

On 2 October some years ago, the three of us decided to visit Raj Ghat. We spent time admiring the tranquillity that Raj Ghat exudes. Mahatma Gandhi is my hero, and I had been waiting for Devaang to reach the age when we could start talking about Gandhi's life, his values and his principles. A visit to Raj Ghat set the stage for our discussion.

Gandhi changed himself, and in the process, changed the world. For him, truth and ahimsa were guiding principles that he adhered to his entire life.

'Setting an example is not the main means of influencing others, it is the only means,' said Albert Einstein. A lady once brought her son to Gandhi. She was worried that he ate too much jaggery, and that it would damage his health. She requested Gandhi to counsel her son about this. Gandhi paused for a moment and then asked the lady to bring her son back after a few days. When they returned, Gandhi told the boy that he shouldn't eat too much jaggery as it could be harmful. The lady was surprised. She asked Gandhi why he had not said this at the first meeting. Gandhi replied, 'I needed a few days to give up eating jaggery so that I could counsel your son with conviction.'

When he started living in an ashram, he expected everyone in the ashram to adhere to the rules. These rules included compliance with moral values, cleaning of toilets, personal hygiene, non-violence, prayer and truth. 'Devaang, when someone digressed, how do you think Mahatma Gandhi reacted? What would most people have done?' 'Punish and set an example so that others do not follow' came the reply. But then, Gandhi was different. He fasted on several occasions because someone in the ashram had lied or stolen or behaved in a manner unbecoming of the high moral standards of the ashram. He did not seek to reprimand or punish. Instead, he chose to appeal to the conscience of those who had sinned by causing himself pain.

He also chose to live in poverty as he was leading people many of whom lived in poverty. Once fond of dressing in the choicest English suits, he preferred to dress himself in a loincloth and shawl. He spun cloth himself and thus made thousands follow him. According to him, 'An ounce of practice is worth more than tons of preaching.'

When Gandhi led the Indian freedom struggle using the principles of ahimsa and satyagraha (a policy of passive political resistance), he knew that there were many who believed that his principles would not help achieve freedom. He didn't expect his views to be accepted immediately. He stressed, 'I will not wait till I have converted the whole society to my view but will straightaway make a beginning with myself' (Gangrade, 2004). With that belief, he won India its independence.

Over the years, Devaang and I have discussed examples from Mahatma Gandhi's life. Whenever I saw an example of tolerance, non-violence or leading by example, I shared it with Devaang. We have watched the movie *Gandhi* on more than one occasion. I often recommend that parents watch this movie with their children.

Children often tend to complain that they do not have enough resources to complete the job at hand. Over the years, I have realized that rather than simply explaining or advising them, I get through better if I can give them an example. The one I love to quote is that of Dashrath Manjhi, who worked as a labourer in a small village in the state of Bihar. His village was next to a mountain, and to reach the closest town, one either had to cross the mountain through a narrow and dangerous pass or travel around the peak. One day, Manjhi's wife was seriously injured trying to cross the mountain. The nearest doctor was 70 km away. Manjhi decided that something needed to be done to shorten the distance between his village and the town. Appeals had been made earlier to the authorities but had not resulted in any action. He was not sure if the villagers were determined enough to find a solution. Manjhi, however, decided that he would be the change he wished to see.

Armed with a hammer, chisel and shovel, he started carving a road through the mountain. He worked alone, night and day. So intense was his determination that he gave up working in the fields to devote all his time to his ambitious project. Manjhi's family had to undergo many hardships as he stopped earning. Many days, he went without food. While he was carving out the road, his wife fell gravely ill. Failing to reach a hospital in time, she passed away. Her loss strengthened Manjhi's resolve. Many villagers thought that Manjhi had lost his mental balance as the task seemed impossible for one man with access to only basic tools. Undeterred, Manjhi soldiered on. In 1982, after twenty-two years of back-breaking hard work and persistence, his road was ready. He created a 360-ft-long and 30-ft-wide road cutting through the mountain. The path, which used to be only a foot wide, now allows cycles and motorcycles to pass, and has transformed the lives of villagers not just in his village but also sixty other villages. His effort cut down the distance from his village to the town from 70 km to 15 km. Dashrath Manjhi achieved what was regarded as near-impossible with no resources at his disposal other than the will to be the change.

I hear about a resource crunch often at work, at social events and, surprisingly, in the clinic. Parents often talk about how children do not get enough individual attention from their teachers because the size of the class is large. 'There is less support for projects because of limited resources,' they say. 'This has an adverse effect on performance,' they add. When children hear their parents highlight the excuses, they learn to use excuses too. I gently mention to parents that while teachers have so many children to take care of, parents have one or two or three children to look after, so why can't more individual attention be given at home? Of the families I see, 95 per cent have less than three children, and 25 per cent have just one child. It is just so convenient to blame others. It is so hard to recognize what we can do.

Subhashini Mistry was one of fourteen children. Seven of her siblings died in childhood. She was married at the age of twelve. Her four children barely survived on her husband's meagre salary. At the age of twenty-three, her husband died for want of proper medical care. Subhashini was distraught. In her sorrow, she took a vow. She would build a hospital for the poor so that others in her circumstances would not have to experience what she did.

The responsibility of raising her four children fell on Subhashini. As she was illiterate, the only job available to her was housework. While she toiled to feed her children, she could not earn enough. She had to keep two of her children in an orphanage. Through all her hardship, she kept thinking about the vow she had taken. After her daughters got married and her elder son started working as a labourer, she realized that to fulfil her dream to build a hospital for the poor, one of her children had to become a doctor. Her youngest child, Ajoy, who had grown up in an orphanage, was a good student. Subhashini encouraged him to study hard and pursue medicine. Ajoy successfully passed the All India Medical Entrance Test and secured admission in Calcutta Medical College. A scholarship allowed him to complete his course. In the meantime, through her savings of twenty years (amounting to Rs 10,000), Subhashini managed to buy a plot of land in her husband's village. Twenty-two years after her husband's death, Subhashini started the Humanity Hospital in a thatched shed. Appeals were made to local doctors to provide free services. Villagers went door-to-door collecting surplus medicines. The first doctor signed on, and 252 patients were seen on the first day. Ajoy sought support from the local member of Parliament (MP) to build a concrete roof for the hospital. The MP came forward to help. Through donations, the Humanity Hospital expanded. It now has two operation theatres and thirty beds spread across 15,000 sq. ft. Twenty-two doctors visit the hospital. This hospital for the poor refuses treatment to none.

We need to share the stories of Dashrath Manjhi and Subhashini Mistry with our children. These are two examples of how common men and women have shown what the spirit of being the change can achieve. There are several other examples that could inspire our children.

Before we ask anyone to change, we need to look inwards. Next time we want our children to be more courteous or gentle or kind, we need to see if we ourselves are well-mannered. Before we reprimand them for being late, we need to think how often we have kept them waiting. We need to make a list of things we should change about ourselves before asking our children to change. We could ask our children to point out the things they would like us to change. We need to be prepared to see a rather long list and unexpected things. When I did this exercise with Devaang, spending quality time and being calmer topped the list. I made an effort to block Sunday afternoons for quality time and made a conscious effort to be calmer. As Devaang saw items on the list being ticked, he came up to me one day and said, 'Dad, will you help me make a list of things I need to change?'

The world is changed by your example, not by your opinion.

— Paulo Coelho

Gratitude

Gratitude unlocks the fullness of life. It turns what we have into enough, and more. It turns denial into acceptance, chaos to order, confusion to clarity. It can turn a meal into a feast, a house into a home, a stranger into a friend.

— Melody Beattie

It was in 2012 that Devaang and I were watching a Grand Slam final. Yet again, Roger Federer had won. 'Dad, isn't Roger Federer amazing? Seventeen Grand Slam singles titles, seven Wimbledon titles, five US Open titles, and 302 weeks at number 1. What an awesome record!'

'How do you remember so many of his records?'

'Federer is my hero! I think he is the greatest player to have ever played the game!'

'He is a legend. His records and qualities are most impressive—hard work, focus, discipline, simplicity, a positive attitude and a remarkable spirit of sportsmanship.

But there is one thing that always stands out for me. Roger understands the power of gratitude.'

'Why gratitude, Dad?'

'Once, at the Australian Open, Federer said, "With all the injury problems we have in men's tennis at the moment, I'm happy to still be standing." Tennis players are at risk of serious injury because of their strenuous lives and the pressure of playing in so many tournaments. The prolonged rehabilitation can make a return to competitive tennis difficult, and several promising careers have ended in premature retirement. Federer realizes that. He has fortunately not had many injuries and he is grateful for that.'

All of us take things for granted. Only when we become unwell do we realize the blessing of good health. As is true of most things, we realize the true value of things only when we have lost them. Our children take so much for granted too— food, clothes, a comfortable bed and toys, a school to go to, vacations to look forward to and birthday parties to enjoy are all considered fixtures. Seldom does a child who has much to be grateful for realize how fortunate he or she is to have what millions of children across the globe can only dream of. We cannot really blame children, as we have not taught them to understand the power of gratitude. They do not see us appreciate the power of gratitude often enough.

'There was another great tennis player who realized the power of gratitude.'

'Who?' asked Devaang.

'Arthur Ashe.'

Ashe was born in Richmond, Virginia. His mother died from complications related to pregnancy at the age of twenty-seven. Ashe and his brother were raised by their father who worked as a handyman.

Ashe started to play tennis at the age of seven. His talent became evident relatively early on, and his father helped him find a coach. Ashe excelled on the tennis court just as he did in the classroom. He graduated first in his class from high school and went on to earn a full scholarship at the University of California, Los Angeles. When he graduated with a degree in business administration, Ashe became the first member on the paternal side of the family to complete college.

In 1968, he won the US Open. He is the only African American man to ever win the US Open. He won the Australian Open two years later and, in 1975, the Wimbledon. He defeated Jimmy Connors at Wimbledon with what is often described as one of the most incredible and improbable victories in the history of modern tennis. Many experts still refer to it as one of the greatest in the history of the tournament. President Ford welcomed Ashe to the White House when he returned home.

He was instrumental in creating the Association of Tennis Professionals (ATP) and later became its president.

Ashe was also a vocal opponent of apartheid and was arrested in Washington during an anti-apartheid protest. He was denied a visa to South Africa and could not play in the South African Open championship. He continued protesting against apartheid over a period of a decade and a half. When Nelson Mandela was set free after twenty-seven years in prison and asked who in the US he wished to have visit him, he said, 'How about Arthur Ashe?'

Ashe suffered a heart attack at the age of thirty-six. Later that year, he had a bypass operation. Four years later, he had a quadruple bypass operation. After his second bypass surgery, he contracted HIV from a blood transfusion. Blood was not screened for HIV at that time. In 1992, he announced that he had AIDS.

His family, friends and colleagues were devastated. From the world over, he received letters from his fans. One fan asked, 'Why does God have to select you for such a bad disease?' To this, Ashe replied: 'The world over, 50 million children start playing tennis, 5 million learn to play tennis, 500,000 learn professional tennis, 50,000 come to the circuit, 5,000 reach the Grand Slam, 50 reach Wimbledon, 4 to the semi-finals and 2 to the finals. When I was holding a cup, I never asked God, "Why me?" And today in pain I should not be asking God, "Why me?"' (Pathak, 2015).

Throughout history, thinkers, philosophers, scientists, statesmen and religious leaders have urged people to understand the power of gratitude. When Devaang was eight months old, he became seriously unwell. He began crying inconsolably and started passing blood. A diagnosis of intussusception was made. In an intussusception, a part of the intestine gets telescoped further into the intestine, resulting in severe symptoms. An intussusception can resolve on its own. As is the case more often, medical or surgical therapy is needed. When he was admitted to hospital, I was still a trainee in paediatrics and had limited understanding of different treatment options. All that Nandini and I could do was to pray for his well-being and leave everything in the hands of the team treating him. We had full faith in the team, and luckily, the intussusception resolved on its own. The whole experience as a father made me realize how hard it is for parents to see their child suffer. As a paediatrician in training, I had not quite realized that parents hold on to every word the treating team utters. As parents, we keenly observed every interaction between Devaang and the nurses. Every blood test and change of cannula caused us much pain. Those days in hospital changed the way I looked at my role and responsibility as a paediatrician. We were so grateful to the team for returning us our baby in good health. I was so grateful to have understood how treatment is seen from the eyes of a parent. That experience changed me as a doctor. From then on, I started thanking every patient I saw. Often my trainees ask me, 'Why do you thank the parents? They are the ones who should thank you.' I try to explain, 'The parents trust me with what is most valuable to them—their child. The least I can do is say thank you. When you become a parent, you will understand better. I did not understand this fact till our son was admitted to hospital.'

Rhonda Byrne in *The Magic* explains that the practice of gratitude is magical and can transform lives (Byrne, 2012). She describes a twenty-eight-day schedule for a magical transformation. Three years ago, I was part of the organizing team for the Second International Congress on Patient Safety in Hyderabad. We decided that in the final session of the conference we would organize a lucky draw to select five delegates who would receive exciting gifts. A day before the conference, we met to decide the prizes. One of our trainees who had registered as a delegate volunteered to help out with a few tasks in the last two sessions. When she learnt that one of the prizes was a BlackBerry phone, she came up to me and said, 'How I wish I could win the BlackBerry.' At the time, I had just read *The Magic* and decided to share what Rhonda Byrne had suggested. I told the young lady, 'Just keep saying thank you for the BlackBerry as if you have won it.' 'How is that going to help me win it?' she asked. 'I have studied science; how can I believe that this will work?' she added. I told her that she would not lose anything by saying thank you.

The final session was from 4:00 p.m. to 5:00 p.m., and at 4:50 p.m., she came up to me and said, 'Please wish me luck. I want that BlackBerry. I have said thank you countless times.' The lucky draw started and the winners were declared one after the other. The final winner was the young lady. As she received her phone, she yelled, 'Saying "thank you" worked!' According to Rhonda Byrne, it works every time. As doctors, we are trained to believe only in data and, at first, I found it hard to understand this idea of expressing gratitude in advance for something one wants and behaving as if one had received it already. After seeing it in practice, I tried expressing gratitude once in advance. It worked—not just once, but every time. I stopped questioning and started believing. Over the years I have shared examples of the power of gratitude with Devaang. Slowly, he too is becoming a believer in the magic of gratitude.

We need to make expression of gratitude a part of our daily lives and the lives of our children. We need to encourage our children to say thank you a little more for the things that they take for granted. When they say thank you many times every day, expressing gratitude then becomes effortless. When our children complain, we need to remind them about what Arthur Ashe had said: 'I should not be asking God "Why me?"'

Let us rise up and be thankful, for if we didn't learn a lot, at least we learned a little, and if we didn't learn a little, at least we didn't get sick, and if we got sick, at least we didn't die; so, let us all be thankful.

— Gautama Buddha

Goals

A goal is a dream with a deadline.

— Napoleon Hill

Are goals really as important as many management gurus make them out to be? Does one need to have goals to become successful? Aren't passion, a burning desire and hard work good enough to achieve success? Management gurus believe that while many qualities are needed for success, goal-setting is perhaps essential to be super successful. Darren Hardy, the author of *Designing the Best 10 Years of Your Life*, makes a compelling case for goal-setting. He believes that nearly 100 per cent of top achievers have two common traits—a relentless commitment to constant learning and clear goals expressed in a document detailing their plans to achieve them. He adds, 'Without goals, your life is like a boat without a rudder. You drift along with the current, inevitably crashing against rocks time and time again. Proper goal-setting puts you in a speedboat and gives you a target to steer towards. You will go directly to your destination and with great speed.'

Many of us have heard of the famous Harvard Business School study about goals. There are those who have found no solid evidence that such a study was conducted, and declare it an urban legend. Urban legend it might be, but the findings were rather interesting. In the book, *What They Don't Teach You at Harvard Business School*, Mark McCormack talks about this study. The graduates of the 1979 MBA programme were asked whether they had clear goals for the future which were written and whether they had plans to accomplish those goals. Only 3 per cent had written goals, 13 per cent had goals that were not written, and 84 per cent had no specific goals. Ten years later, the class was interviewed again. The 13 per cent who had unwritten goals were earning twice as much as the 84 per cent with no goals. And the 3 per cent who had written down their goals were earning ten times more than 97 per cent of their batchmates. While this study looked at only earning, experts believe that written goals for other aspects—spiritual, mental or physical (weight loss, exercising and so on)—result in a greater chance of success (McCormack, 2014).

If we subscribe to the concept of the need for well-defined goals, it would seem logical that we would want to sensitize our children to goal-setting. It is, however, very hard for children to understand this concept. One way is to share stories with children on how well-defined goals have made the impossible possible. The stories need to be chosen based on the child's interest. As Devaang—like most children—found stories about space travel interesting, I made an attempt to link goal-setting with a space odyssey. Space programmes across the world are shining examples of what clearly spelt-out goals can achieve.

On 25 May 1961, President John F. Kennedy told the Congress, 'I believe this nation should commit itself to achieving the goal, before this decade is out, of landing a man on the moon and returning him safely to earth. No single space project in this period will be more impressive to mankind, or more important for the long-range exploration of space; and none will be so difficult or expensive to accomplish' (Kennedy, 1961). The National Aeronautics and Space Administration (NASA) took on the challenge.

The goal was indeed difficult and expensive. The estimated cost was USD 20 billion. Coordination of an order that had never been seen before was needed—design, redesign procurement, engineering, construction, manufacturing, training, retraining, testing, retesting, logistics and operations. More than 500 contractors and 250 subcontractors were commissioned. Scientists, engineers, academics and managers from all over the US came together as one team with one goal. Millions of components were procured. Important questions such as the method of going to the moon—direct ascent, earth orbit rendezvous (with the need for a space station for the rendezvous) or lunar orbit rendezvous (using a small lander to land on the lunar surface)—needed to be answered. The three critical factors of schedule, reliability and cost were addressed together as they were interrelated. The timeline was clear—a decade. As human lives were involved, reliability was important to ensure safety. Costs needed to be contained, and any delay would result in an increase in cost (see http://history.nasa.gov/Apollomon/Apollo.html#note30).

The mission needed immaculate planning and several milestones had to be crossed. The first was an orbital flight with an astronaut. On 20 February 1962, John Glenn circled the earth in the Friendship 7 Mercury spacecraft. The second was to perform a spacewalk which was achieved through Project Gemini by 1966. The third was to gain more knowledge about the moon through satellites. Project Ranger, Lunar Orbiter and Project Surveyor provided the information that was needed. The fourth was the ability to reliably launch the mission using boosters. The Saturn boosters after fifteen launches scored 100 per cent on reliability. Tragedy, however, struck on 27 January 1967. Three astronauts who were to fly on Apollo Saturn died when a fire broke out during a mock launch. Finally, on 16 July 1969, Apollo 11 lifted off. On 20 July 1969, Neil Armstrong set foot on the moon and half a billion people watched him make history and utter the famous words, 'That's one small step for [a] man and one giant leap for mankind.' The goal of landing a man on the moon and bringing him back safely had been achieved in a little over eight years because thousands of individuals came together and put everything else aside to achieve that goal.

While the first few decades of space exploration saw intense rivalry between Russia and the US to achieve supremacy, the International Space Station (ISS) showed how cooperation could be achieved between competitors in the pursuit of a common goal. The Russian MIR-Z space station and American Freedom project were brought together in 1993. The ISS has five collaborations—NASA, the Russian

Federal Space Agency (ROSKOSMOS), the European Space Agency (ESA), the Japanese Aerospace Exploration Agency (JAXA) and the Canadian Space Agency (CSA). The station has two sections—one Russian and one American—330 km above earth. Astronauts of all nationalities use the Russian Soyuz rockets to reach the ISS. Cooperation of the degree seen today would have been unimaginable four decades ago. All this was made possible by a common goal.

The Indian Space Research Organisation (ISRO) brought together Indians from across the world to achieve well-defined goals—launch of India's first satellite Aryabhatta in 1975, vehicles to launch multiple satellites in a single mission and launch of the lunar probe Chandrayaan in 2008. The Mars Orbiter Mission (MOM) was launched in 2013 with the goal of becoming the first in the world to enter the Martian orbit in its maiden attempt.

On an individual level, Elbert Leander 'Burt' Rutan set a goal of creating a privately funded spacecraft to make space travel affordable. Rutan built SpaceShip One at a cost of just USD 25 million. He thus made it possible for the first two individuals who were not part of a government-funded programme to go into space.

Every news report, book, TV programme and film on space provided me with an opportunity to share the power of a goal with Devaang using the excitement space travel generated in him.

When we visited Singapore for a holiday, Devaang kept marvelling at the cleanliness, the sense of order and civility he observed there. 'This is such a remarkable country. How have they been able to do so well?' he asked. 'Singaporeans have

Mr Lee Kuan Yew to thank. He had an aim, and he achieved it,' was my response.

Lee Kuan Yew is recognized globally as the founding father of Singapore. Lee became the first prime minister of Singapore in 1959 (see Cavendish, 2009). Following Singapore's separation from Malaysia in 1965, the Republic of Singapore was created. With an area of 241 sq. miles and a population of 1.879 million, Singapore had no natural resources and limited capability to defend itself. Transforming Singapore from a developing to a developed country was the goal Lee set out to achieve. Detailed plans and policies were created. In his book *From Third World to First: The Singapore Story*, he shared the transformation (Yew, 2000). To strengthen defence capabilities, conscription was introduced. Male citizens were asked to serve in the armed forces, police or civil defence force. Tolerance to a multicultural, multi-religious way of life was encouraged. There was zero tolerance for corruption. To ensure an honest administration, salaries of officials were linked to salaries in the private sector. Lee believed that Singapore's people were its biggest asset, and their work ethic would draw businessmen from around the world. A strong legal system, transparency and investor-friendly and business-conducive policies resulted in Singapore becoming a preferred business destination. Recognized globally for his statesmanship, Lee received many awards, including the Lincoln Medal, an award reserved for people who have exemplified the legacy and character embodied by Abraham Lincoln.

In 2009, I was on my way back from a lecture tour in Africa. The flight had a stopover in Kigali, the capital of Rwanda. On the flight from Kigali to Doha, an engineer from Rwanda was my companion. As I had read about the rapid strides his country had made, I asked him a lot of questions about life in Rwanda. In the few hours we spent together, he shared an amazing story, one that I had a chance to pass on to Devaang.

In 1994, Rwanda saw a genocide that wiped out 10 per cent of its population. Paul Kagame became the President of Rwanda in 2000. After he was sworn in, Kagame created Rwanda's vision of 2020 goals. The goals were good governance; an efficient state; skilled human capital, including education, health and information technology; a vibrant private sector; world-class physical infrastructure; modern agriculture and livestock. Kagame aimed to decrease the number of people living in poverty by half and increase average annual earnings from USD 237 to USD 900. He set about achieving his goals through pragmatic policies. Today, the Rwanda Parliament has more women than men, controlling corruption has received much attention and Rwanda has gone from rank 83 to 49 in a list of 177 countries on the corruption index in less than ten years. It is also the fifty-second country on the World Bank's list of 200 best countries to do business with. Cleanliness drives, a national health insurance programme and better literacy rates have changed the face of the country. More than 200,000 children in the country have received laptops as Kagame has set his sights on making Rwanda a knowledge economy. Such is the sense of pride that he has instilled in young citizens that they want to study and work not just for their own benefit but also for the betterment of their country. Observers have started referring to Rwanda as the 'Singapore of Africa'.

Over the years, Devaang has learnt more about how a goal can transform countries. It has shown him that if a goal can have such an impact on a large scale, it can do wonders at an individual level.

Every week, I see children with serious liver problems. Their parents are willing to move heaven and earth to see their children get better. One person who stands out in my memory is the mother of one of my patients, Vinay. She had one goal: to see her son get a new lease of life. As an eleven-year-old, Vinay was referred to Apollo Hospital, Delhi, for a liver transplant. He suffered from an uncommon liver disease called primary sclerosing cholangitis. In this disease, the bile ducts get progressively scarred and liver failure develops. When end-stage liver failure is established, the only treatment is a liver transplant. I distinctly remember the first time I saw Vinay. He looked thin and weak. He was carrying a big bag that had a tube connected to his gall bladder to drain bile. He had a huge smile and his eyes were extremely expressive. The smile was something that pleasantly surprised me. Vinay had been in a hospital for months and several endoscopic procedures had been performed on him. He had missed a year of school and had not interacted with his friends for a long time. No sports, no fun and a life confined to a hospital bed. Yet, he was smiling.

As we started preparing for the transplant, it became clear that the social and economic situation of the family was going to pose challenges. Vinay's mother was the sole breadwinner, with three children to support. She also wanted to donate a part of her liver. She was devastated when she was rejected as a donor (her liver was found to be unsuitable). The father had a matching blood group, but he was an alcoholic and had given up work. We mentioned to the father that he could be a suitable donor if he gave up alcohol. The mother told us to leave it to her to get her husband to give up alcohol. Our hospital and team had offered to perform a free transplant, but we still needed to raise Rs 6 lakh for the consumables and medicines. We wrote to the Chief Minister's Relief Fund. Two of our patients agreed to make a contribution for Vinay's transplant. As we worked on raising funds, we were encouraged to see Vinay's father refraining from alcohol. Three months later, he was declared fit to be a donor. By that time, we had raised Rs 5 lakh and still needed Rs 1 lakh. The village panchayat decided to help out by organizing kabaddi matches in neighbouring villages. The funds thus needed were raised, and his father donated the right lobe of his liver. Vinay recovered and was discharged in two weeks. He remains healthy and is doing well at school. His father now works as a carpenter and has not touched alcohol for years.

If we want our children to benefit from goals, we need to start working with our children at a young age to help them set goals. We could start with one small goal, and once that is achieved, a bigger goal may be set. For example, if a child does not like mathematics, there is no point in setting a goal of achieving an A grade in the next assessment. Setting a goal of enjoying mathematics by making it more interesting would be more helpful. Once the child finds mathematics interesting, he or she herself will aim to improve his or her grades and in time realize the value of goal-setting.

Mohamed El-Erian served as the CEO of a large investment fund and made USD 100 million a year. El-Erian resigned from his position when his ten-year-old daughter listed twenty-two milestones in her life he had missed because of work. In an article written by Cahal Milmo in the *Independent*, El-Erian was quoted: 'I felt awful and got defensive; I had a good excuse for each missed event! Travel, important meetings, an urgent phone call, sudden to-dos. But it dawned on me that I was missing an infinitely more important point. As much as I could rationalize it, my work–life balance had gotten way out of whack, and the imbalance was hurting my relationship with my daughter' (Milmo, 2014). Mohamed El-Erian now has a new goal— rebuilding his relationship with his daughter. We should learn from El-Erian, and, as parents, start with one goal: to spend quality time with our children. If we can make this goal specific, measurable and timeline-bound, we can make a huge positive difference to our relationship with our children.

Goals can take men to where no man has gone before, make adversaries cooperate, transform nations, change lives and save lives, so why are we waiting to acquaint our children with the magic of goals?

Arise! Awake! And stop not until the goal is reached.

— Swami Vivekananda

Honesty

No legacy is so rich as honesty.

— William Shakespeare

We often talk about honesty. At work and at home, we lecture one another about honesty. We want our children to be honest. We parents often forget that young children are honest. They do not lie. They do not steal. They are not dishonest, as they have not been exposed to dishonesty. As they grow up, they see examples of it around them.

One of my little patients, Aadil, has such a beautiful smile that it can turn anybody's regular day into a special day. Whenever Aadil enters my room with that smile, he brings along so much joy. On one visit, when I was about to say bye to him after the consultation, he whispered something into his mother Smita's ear and then said, 'injection'. I was surprised to hear that, as Aadil was not scheduled to receive a vaccine that day. I asked his mother why he was mentioning an injection. What Smita said made me smile. 'Aadil has become a fussy eater, and I had warned him that if he doesn't start eating properly, he will get an injection from the doctor,' she said. When Aadil realized that the examination was over and his mother had forgotten to ask the doctor to give him an injection, he reminded his mother. At the age of four, he knew very well that injections hurt, yet he reminded his mother about it. I have rarely seen an act of such pure honesty.

We as parents need to remember that while we cannot always prevent exposure to dishonesty outside our homes, at home, we need to be role models. We need to emphasize the value of honesty through our conduct. We need to encourage a discussion on what is honest and what is not, as often as we can. Asking for medical leave from school so that a child can go for a family function is dishonest. Getting someone else to do a child's homework is dishonest. Neither can happen without the approval or support of parents. I have noticed over the years the emergence of 'holiday project services'. In order to keep their students occupied meaningfully during the summer vacation, schools prescribe holiday projects. The idea behind these projects is to encourage students to think about issues beyond books. The scale and degree of complexity of the projects can vary. Some parents do not want or do not have the time to work with their child on the holiday projects. Sensing an opportunity, agencies have sprung up to complete holiday projects. For a fee, simple or complex holiday projects can be delivered at one's doorstep. When parents make use of such services, they perhaps do not realize that by encouraging this practice, they have introduced their child to dishonesty.

A story that exemplifies the virtue of honesty is one of my favourites. There was once a Chinese emperor who had no children. He asked for thousands of children to be brought to his palace. He then announced that one of those children would be chosen as his successor. He gave every child a seed and asked the children to go back to their homes, plant the seed in a pot and look after it. He told them that he would assess their effort a year later and chose his heir.

All the children started tending to the seed that had been given to them. There was a little boy whose pot despite being watered every day showed no sign of life. Weeks passed and the little boy's pot remained just as it was, while the pots of other children started to sprout flowers and shrubs. The little boy was disappointed but kept watering the pot every day. A year went by and his pot remained barren. As the time to meet the emperor came, the little boy started to worry that he would be ridiculed as only his pot was bereft of life. His mother told him that as the emperor wanted to see all the pots, he would need to go irrespective of the consequences. The little boy went to the palace and felt ashamed at his inadequacy, as all the other pots looked beautiful with magnificent plants. The emperor started to inspect all the pots. When he saw the barren pot, he asked the little boy what had happened. The little boy replied, 'Your Majesty, I cared for the seed and watered it every day for one year, but nothing happened.' After he had inspected all the pots, the emperor said, 'Last year I gave you all seeds. All the seeds had been boiled, so they were useless. As I see all the beautiful flowers and plants, I realize that all of you substituted the seeds I gave you when you saw that there was no sign of life. Only this little boy with a barren pot has displayed integrity which I believe is the most important virtue of leadership. He, therefore, shall be my heir.'

While we should lead by example, we also need to share examples of honesty with children.

Lal Bahadur Shastri served as prime minister of India for a rather brief period from 1964 to 1966. He was an exceptional leader whose simplicity and integrity made him stand out as a statesman. Born on the same day as Mahatma Gandhi, Lal Bahadur Shastri was his devoted disciple. He was arrested several times by the British during India's freedom struggle. Once, he was granted permission to spend fifteen days with his sick daughter. By the time he reached home, his daughter had unfortunately died. He performed the last rites and, three days later, returned to prison even though he could have stayed on for twelve more days. On another occasion, he was given seven days of furlough from prison to tend to his ailing son. Although his son continued to remain seriously ill, Shastri returned to prison on the completion of seven days.

Another statesman known for his honesty was Abraham Lincoln. When Lincoln worked as store clerk in New Salem, he earned the title of 'Honest Abe'. He once walked several miles to return extra pennies he had charged a customer by mistake. On another occasion, a customer bought half a pound of tea but received only a quarter pound as the weighing scale was faulty. Lincoln closed the store and walked a fair distance to deliver the other quarter pound of tea.

Word about his honesty spread, and he was held in high esteem by everyone. In an election for the Senate, Lincoln lost to Stephen Douglas. Two years later, Lincoln and Douglas fought for the presidency. When Douglas was informed that Lincoln had won, he said to the person who broke the news, 'You have nominated a very able and very honest man.'

Sports is an arena wherein honesty is of the highest importance, as sports without fair play loses all its sheen.

Bobby Jones was the first golfer to win four major tournaments in a single year. In one national championship, Bobby drove his ball into the woods and accidentally nudged it. Even though no one had seen him nudge the ball, he penalized himself and lost the game by a stroke. When everyone praised him for his integrity, he said, 'You might as well praise a man for not robbing a bank.'

In an athletics event in 2012, Ivan Fernandez Anaya saw Abel Mutai who was leading the cross-country race pull up about 10 metres before the finish line in the mistaken belief that he had crossed the line. Anaya could have easily benefited by going ahead, but instead, he stayed behind and through gestures, guided Mutai to cross the finishing line first.

On graduating, doctors take the Hippocratic oath. The oath serves to instil in a doctor the need to adhere to several core values at all times. Honesty is one such value: honesty in professional relationships with colleagues and honesty in the doctor–patient relationship. As a paediatrician, breaking catastrophic news to parents is very difficult. To tell parents that they are going to lose their child is to my mind the hardest task a paediatrician faces. While one can choose gentle words, expressions and phrases, a paediatrician has to be honest even though it is easier to paint a rosy picture. Even if hope is all that keeps both the family and the doctor going, one has to be realistic and absolutely honest. What I have discovered is that when things are going downhill, parents—perceptive as they are—can sense it. If parents know that everything possible has been done, they slowly accept the reality of loss. I distinctly remember having a difficult conversation with Sheena and Neepesh, the parents of baby Evaan, who needed a liver transplant but was unfortunately suffering from multiple other problems, which did not allow us to go ahead with the operation. The baby had been referred to Apollo Hospital from Kenya for a transplant. When we lost Evaan, the whole team felt really sad as we had become attached to him. We had been honest in sharing our assessment and the family was deeply appreciative of this approach. They felt that our honesty had helped them prepare for the inevitable. They wrote a beautiful card, thanking us for keeping him as comfortable as we could in his final days. Sheena set up a foundation in Evaan's memory and requested me to join the advisory board. Rakhi and Adish Oswal, who lost a baby waiting for a liver transplant, were very appreciative of the honest approach. They support an annual academic programme at our centre in the memory of their son, Kunwar Viren Oswal. They even christened their daughter with the name I had picked for her.

Whenever I have to break news about the deterioration in a child's condition, it shows on my face. No matter how hard I try not to take the load home, I fail. When Nandini and Devaang see me looking glum, they ask me what is going on. As I cannot discuss details because of patient confidentiality, all I can say is, 'It is not easy being honest when you have to share devastating news.' The message I hope to pass on to

Devaang is that just because it is tough it does not mean we should take an easier route.

Honesty and integrity are often used interchangeably, but they are different. There can be honesty without integrity, but no integrity without honesty. Honesty has to do with being truthful and upfront, while integrity is doing what is right without worrying about the consequences. Subroto Bagchi in his book *The Professional* describes integrity quite simply: 'We follow the rules. Where rules do not exist, we use fair judgement. When in doubt, we do not go ahead and do what suits us; we seek counsel. If faced with a dilemma, we ask ourselves: can my act stand public scrutiny without causing embarrassment to me and my family?' (Bagchi, 2010). This description addresses a complex issue in a manner simple enough for a child to understand.

In each of our hospitals, we present honesty awards on our Annual Day. Staff members who have displayed honesty are honoured. I distinctively remember one security guard who was awarded for returning an iPhone, a laptop and USD 10,000 that a foreign patient had misplaced. What this young lady returned was more than her salary for several months, but she did not think twice before doing what was right. I make it a point to talk about these awards with Devaang to reinforce the point that there are a lot of honest people. We just need to keep our eyes open.

In the north-eastern state of Mizoram, there is a remarkable example of honesty. Along the highway to the capital, Aizawl, are several shops referred to as *Nghah lou dawr* shops. These shops have no shopkeepers. The shop owners display vegetables, fruits and flowers along with a rate list. Next to the rate list is a container into which customers are supposed to drop the money. The customers choose what they want to buy, calculate what is due using the rate list and leave the money in the container. This business works on trust and has for decades. It is a living example of communities adhering to integrity in a world where this virtue is rare to find. Albert Camus had said, 'Integrity needs no rules.' This certainly holds true in Mizoram at the *Nghah lou dawr* shops.

When we see our children display honesty, we should be lavish in our praise. Praise can serve as positive conditioning that encourages a child to repeat behaviour that earns him or her praise. When that behaviour is repeated several times, it is becomes a part of the child's nature.

Every time we get tempted to take the path leading away from honesty, we should remind ourselves about incidents from the lives of Abraham Lincoln, Lal Bahadur Shastri, Bobby Jones and Ivan Fernandez Anaya. We should look around and appreciate ordinary men and women who display extraordinary honesty. If we follow the path of honesty, so will our children.

Honesty is more than not lying. It is truth telling, truth speaking, truth living, and truth loving.

— James E. Faust

Forgiveness

Forgiveness is the fragrance that the violet sheds on the heel that has crushed it.

— Mark Twain

Forgiveness is a virtue that is very hard to practise. Each one of us has had bitter experiences, and the pain, suffering and hurt vividly stands out in one's memory. It is just so hard to forget, let alone forgive.

I had been struggling with ideas on how to begin a conversation with Devaang about forgiveness. In 2010, we were watching the inaugural ceremony of the FIFA World Cup. Nelson Mandela seemed so happy. He had brought the FIFA World Cup to South Africa in the hope that it would help establish South Africa as a democratic nation where diversity was respected and discrimination based on colour was a thing of the past. It dawned on me that now was the opportunity. Who could provide a better example of forgiveness than Nelson Mandela?

When Mandela was tried for treason in 1956, he was sent to the maximum security prison on Robben Island, 5 miles offshore from Cape Town. Several protestors against apartheid were jailed on Robben Island. His cell was 7 feet by 9 feet and had no bed. In his book, *Long Walk to Freedom*, Mandela recounts, 'I would walk the length of my cell in three paces. When I lay down, I could feel the wall with my feet, and my head grazed the concrete at the other side' (Mandela, 1995). He was a class D prisoner (lowest category), so he could have only one visitor every six months. He was allowed to write or receive a letter once in six months. The letter too was censored. He was, in effect, cut off from the world.

Mandela was assigned the job of breaking rocks at the limestone quarry. The limestone dust caused lung damage, and the harsh sunlight affected his eyesight. When his eldest son died in a car accident, he was denied permission to attend the funeral. After eighteen years, he was transferred from the Robben Island prison to the Pollsmoor prison and then the Victor Verster prison. As the 'Free Nelson Mandela' campaign gained momentum, Mandela was finally released after twenty-seven years in prison at the age of seventy-two.

Mandela displayed no anger towards his oppressors. He showed no bitterness for the hard times in prison. He was asked how he could forget the terrible years in prison. Didn't the decades of suffering make him angry? How could he keep hatred in check? He replied, 'Hating clouds the mind. It gets in the way of strategy. Leaders cannot afford to hate.'

Soon after his release, he led the African National Congress to victory in the first multiracial election. He became South Africa's first black president. F.W. de Klerk, who as president had ordered his release, became the first deputy president.

Mandela thought along the same lines as Mahatma Gandhi who said, 'An eye for an eye leaves the whole world blind.' For his inauguration, he invited Paul Gregory who had served as a prison warden in Robben Island prison. He dedicated his time to building trust between the black and white South Africans using the power of forgiveness. He invited Percy Yutar, the prosecutor who had demanded the death penalty for Mandela in 1956, for a meal. After the meeting, Mandela commented that Yutar had only been doing his job when he pushed for the death penalty.

Mandela wanted South Africa to become a 'rainbow nation' that took pride in its diversity. He reassured the white minority that they would be protected, while ensuring that the black majority would finally get what was due after decades of struggle. He made sure that his personal staff and security team comprised both black and white South Africans. He realized that the distrust and the scars of oppression would take time to overcome.

A few weeks after the inauguration ceremony of the FIFA World Cup, Devaang and I went to a video store. I noticed the CD of the film *Invictus* on the shelf. As children need reinforcement to imbibe the values we want them to nurture, I decided to buy the video to give us another opportunity to talk about Mandela.

Invictus, which in Latin means 'undefeated' or 'unconquered', is a poem written by William Earnest Henly. It inspired Mandela in jail for twenty-seven years, giving him the strength to remain unconquered despite the seclusion and oppression.

The movie recounts the story of how Mandela used a sport to bring together a nation. Mandela knew that the blacks did not support the mostly white national rugby union team called Springboks. Whenever Springboks played in South Africa, the black community would support the opposition. Mandela believed that rugby could serve as the balm the two communities needed. The Rugby World Cup was to be hosted by South Africa in 1995. Mandela urged the black-dominated South African Sports Committee formed post apartheid to lend their support to Springboks. Many were opposed to the idea, but Mandela persevered. He met with the captain of Springboks, Francois Pienaar, and shared his dream of a Springboks victory bringing the two communities together and uniting South Africa. As the team started interacting with the fans, the unimaginable happened. The support for Springboks in the black population grew as the tournament progressed, and South Africa defeated New Zealand in the final. Mandela presented the cup to Pienaar, wearing a green Springboks jersey bearing Pienaar's number '6'. This event did more for reconciliation than even Mandela could have hoped for. De Klerk later said, 'Mandela won the hearts of millions of white rugby fans' (Pettinger, 2013). The Rugby World Cup final helped put the past behind.

Mandela continued to win hearts long after he stepped down from office. He offered a scholarship to the son of one of his prison wardens, Christo Brand.

The 'founding father of democracy' left behind a united South Africa where everyone has equal rights. He left the world with the most powerful message of forgiveness. Scott Johnson wrote in *Smithsonian Magazine* that Zozo, a former prisoner at Robben Island and now a tour guide, told him, 'Our leader Nelson Mandela taught us not to take revenge on our enemies. And because of this, today we are free, free, free' (Johnson, 2012). As we ended our discussion, I said to Devaang, 'That is why Nelson Mandela's example will be given to generations that follow.'

Throughout history, there have been astonishing and heart-rending examples of forgiveness.

British MP Anthony Berry died in a bomb blast planned by the Irish Republic Army in Brighton in 1984. The bomb had been planted by Patrick Magee. Berry's daughter, Jo, tried to come to terms with her loss. She did not want to become bitter, and immersed herself in conflict mediation. When Magee was released from prison in 1999 as part of the Good Friday Agreement, Jo expressed a desire to meet him. The meeting lasted for three hours. They met again, and after several meetings and many conversations, they became friends. Jo forgave Magee. Together, they decided to spread the message across the globe about healing and forgiveness.

During the Vietnam War, Napalm bombs dropped by the US caused devastation. A young girl, Kim Phuc, was severely injured during one such attack. A photo of Kim received a lot of media attention that served to highlight the ravages of the Vietnam War. Kim lost some of her family members in that attack. She had to undergo seventeen surgeries as a result of the injuries she sustained. Yet, she displayed no bitterness. She was willing to forgive those who were responsible for the pain and suffering. In 1996, she met the pilot who had led the attack at the Vietnam Veterans Memorial in Washington, DC and forgave him in person.

When we visited Jallianwala Bagh in Amritsar where approximately 1,000 defenceless Indians were massacred by the British, Devaang asked us, 'Why were Indians so tolerant? Why did they not hate the British?' I replied, 'Son, we were fortunate to have someone who showed us the path of tolerance, non-violence and forgiveness.'

Gandhi saw the British rulers divide his countrymen. He saw a land as rich as India brought to economic ruin. He saw the agony of losing family members when he met with the families of those who had been massacred at Jallianwala Bagh. He himself underwent enormous hardship in prison for several years. Yet, he had no anger towards the British. In his famous 'Quit India' speech, where he asked the British to leave and launched the Quit India movement, he shared his feelings about the British: 'There is the question of your attitude towards the British. I have noticed that there is hatred towards the British among the people. The people say they are disgusted with their behaviour. We must get rid of this feeling. Our quarrel is not with the British people; we fight their imperialism. . . . At a time when I may have to launch the biggest struggle of my life, I may not harbour hatred against anybody' (Gandhi, 1942).

Children need help to realize the power of forgiveness. I remember the case of a twelve-year-old boy who was brought in with complaints of tiredness. He had no other physical symptoms. Children are often brought for consultation for a physical manifestation which turns out to have a psychological cause. When I asked questions pertaining to his psychological health and well-being, the parents mentioned that the boy was unable to complete his homework, did not enjoy games and seemed unhappy. He got angry often and just seemed disinterested in everything, including studies. On probing further, it became clear that the behavioural change started after an incident at school.

The boy had had a fight with a classmate and the teacher had taken the fighting duo to the headmaster. The boy was reprimanded and had since developed problems. The boy felt that while he had not started the fight, he had been held equally responsible. He was angry at the child who started the fight, the teacher and the headmaster. This incident had taken place two months before. The parents had held meetings with the parents of the other child, the teacher and the headmaster to understand what exactly had happened. The boy had been selected to represent the school in a declamation contest. His classmate who had not been selected had come to the boy's desk to tell him that he did not deserve to be selected. An argument had ensued, and the child who had not been selected slapped the boy. The boy slapped him back, and it turned into a full-fledged fight, with the class teacher separating the two boys. The boy felt that he had been treated unfairly as he had not started the fight but had only retaliated. No disciplinary action other than a letter to the two boys had been issued. The headmaster and teacher felt that the boy was making too much of the incident. The boy could just not get over the incident, and it started seriously affecting his life. Over a course of three consultations, the boy realized that it was only he who was suffering, and for him to move on, he needed to forgive his classmate for what he had done. It took considerable counselling for the boy to finally agree that forgiveness was the answer. He eventually forgave and moved on. His grades became what they were before the incident, and he started to enjoy his favourite sport again and became cheerful.

Forgiveness is indeed powerful. It can provide closure. We have to rid ourselves and our children of the misconception that it makes the person small. It actually makes the person bigger. Mahatma Gandhi believed, 'The weak can never forgive. Forgiveness is the attribute of the strong.' If our children see us forgiving those who have wronged us, so will they. If our children see us becoming bitter and seeking revenge, so will they.

To forgive is to set a prisoner free and discover that the prisoner was you.

— Lewis B. Smedes

Conclusion

In eighteen chapters, I have tried to capture what I believe are the essential values to prepare our children to face the world. Some of these virtues might be more important than others. I have not categorized them in order of importance, and neither have I suggested an ideal order in which to share these with children. Some are harder than others to inculcate. Each virtue, however easy it might seem, needs reinforcement and conditioning.

I found access to technology helpful in making the interactions with Devaang more engaging and lively. The Internet, Wikipedia and YouTube were useful tools. Movies, books and magazines were helpful, as were visits to museums and monuments. Spontaneity and fun were essential ingredients.

While the purpose of my experiment was to teach Devaang without formally lecturing him, I learnt so much myself. In many ways, the learning changed me as a person.

Over the years, I learnt a lot about parenting by observing relatives, friends and parents of patients. I learnt the power of encouragement when I saw Anubha and Tapesh Bagati encourage their son Arhan to create an app for athletes for the

Rio Paralympics. I learnt the power of caring when I saw Silvia and Anup Soni teach their children Ishana and Armaan how to care for their sibling. I learnt the power of reasoning with a seven-year-old when I saw Mumtaz and Irfan Siddiqui explain the importance of vaccination to their twins Miriam and Zayra. I learnt that children hate to be compared to siblings, relatives, classmates, neighbours and friends. Comparisons lead to negativity. I learnt that to reprimand a child for a mistake is detrimental; a logical discussion is more useful. Trying to pass a judgement is damaging. I learnt that parents need to strictly avoid adding the pressure of performance in the already stressful pressure-cooker-like environment children find themselves in today. I learnt that encouragement, praise, motivation, suggestions, patience (loads of it) and a gentle nudge (rather than a push) work, sometimes better than one would expect. I learnt that for a child to embrace an idea, a virtue or a skill, a parent has to generate an eager want in the child. A child will only do what he or she wants. As simple as that. The key is to create that want.

Devaang shared his worries, hopes, dreams, confusion, joys and sorrows more and more as we went down this exciting path of learning and growth. I too shared my feelings in a manner that I had not thought possible. Devaang and I became friends—for life.

Whatever I have discussed so far I have summarized as eighteen virtues and fifty dos and don'ts.

1. Humility
+ Parents themselves should be humble so that children can observe humility at close quarters.

- We need to start early as this virtue takes a long time to develop.
- Humility paves the way for other virtues.

2. **Beating the Odds**
   - Parents themselves should not make excuses for not being able to do something.
   - When our children do so, we should share examples that make their excuses look lame.
   - We should ask our children to identify those who have overcome challenges.

3. **It's Never Too Late**
   - Every minute brings with it sixty seconds, every day 1,440 minutes and every year 8,760 hours of an opportunity to change. So it is never too late.

4. **Courage**
   - Parents should applaud every act of courage, no matter how small.
   - Repeated praise conditions the mind to aim higher and gives the body the strength to push harder.

5. **Handling Pressure**
   - We should not add to the pressure kids are already handling.
   - Parents should handle pressure better.
   - Some amount of pressure is inevitable, so we need to help our children learn to feed off it.

6. **Making Mistakes, Accepting Flaws**
   - No parent is perfect, so we shouldn't expect our children to be perfect.
   - Every mistake is a lesson; parents and children must learn together.
   - We need to avoid being judgemental as that can destroy a parent–child relationship.
   - We must offer unconditional love.

7. **Be a Dreamer**
   - Parents need to encourage children to dream.
   - We should help fulfil the dreams of our children to the greatest extent possible.
   - We must not kill our child's dream.
   - Parents should not expect their children to fulfil their (parents') dreams.

8. **Find Your Calling**
   - We need to guide our children to discover their calling.
   - Just because a child wants to do something different, he or she should not be discouraged.
   - Children need not follow the herd as they are distinct individuals with a unique genetic makeup who don't need to conform to perceived norms.

9. **Compassion**
   - Parents can learn compassion from children.
   - We should not use our limited concept of compassion to influence our children.
   - Every act of compassion should be rewarded.

10. Making Others Happy

- It is our job to make our children happy. We signed up for it when we became parents.

- Parents should not expect their children to make them happy; they did not sign up for that.

- We should try and make everyone around us happy, to spread the joy to our children and ourselves.

11. Never Give Up Hope

- No matter how down and out our children might feel, we must always offer hope.

- A child will come to us at times as the last resort. If we do not offer hope, who will?

12. Determination

- As life is full of ups and downs, we need to drive home the virtue of perseverance.

- Our children should see determination in us to draw strength from us.

- Every time a child falls, parents should offer a helping hand and help him stand up once again.

13. Giving

- We should help our children discover the joy of giving.

- Parents of boys have to start earlier and try harder.

- Every time a child gives something without the desire to be seen giving, we must be lavish in our praise.

- If we can give without seeking recognition ourselves, giving will then become a way of life for the family.

14. Be the Change

- If parents themselves do not want to change, they should not expect any change in their children.
- If our children see us change, they will want to do the same.

15. Gratitude

- Many of us are not as grateful as we should be for all that we have.
- We need to shift focus from what we do not have to what we have as a family.
- When we do that as a family, our children too will follow.

16. Goals

- We must create goals for ourselves as parents.
- We should involve our children in this goal-setting exercise.
- When our children see goal(s) being met, they will embrace the magic of goals.

17. Honesty

- Parents need to be role models.
- We need to provide such a strong atmosphere of honesty at home that our children shun dishonesty, which they will invariably get exposed to in the world.

18. Forgiveness

- Forgiveness is a very powerful virtue, but very hard to inculcate.

- Unless our children see us forget and forgive, and that too frequently, they will find it very hard to even try to walk down the path of forgiveness.

I realized that if Devaang was to believe in the values I wanted to instil in him, I needed to walk the talk. Talking alone would not serve the purpose; action would be needed.

When you thought I wasn't looking,
I saw that you cared,
and I wanted to be everything that I could be.

— Mary Rita Schilke Korazan
'When You Thought I Wasn't Looking'

Acknowledgements

I would like to thank my parents for a great childhood.

Dad, thank you for all the lessons delivered with so much clarity and simplicity. 'Never believe anything you hear about yourself, unless it is said to your face', 'Don't say something unless you are comfortable with it being repeated', 'Always try to share others' sorrows; sharing their joy is optional', 'Never start a business with a friend', 'Be calm when there is a crisis', 'Give every assignment your all without worrying about the result', 'You are not a bag of salt that you will get soggy' (when at the age of eight I did not come to fetch your briefcase as I always did because it was raining that day) are just a handful of the many lessons that you taught me that shaped my thinking.

Mom, thank you for your unconditional love. I have always known that you will support me 100 per cent at all times. I have tried to do a bit of what you did for me, for your grandson.

A big thank you to my in-laws for letting me marry their lovely daughter and for being more like friends than in-laws. Thanks Ma and Pa for all the advice you gave as I bounced off ideas about the book.

Thank you Nandini for sharing your life with me, for encouraging me through medical college and the eleven years of training, for never asking for anything, for being ever so accommodating and for raising Devaang the way you have. If it was not for your support, this book would never have been written.

Thank you Devaang. If it wasn't for you, there would have been no book.

Thank you Dr Reddy for being such an inspirational leader. Several virtues I have alluded to in this book I see in you.

Thank you Mrs Reddy for your many acts of compassion that I have had the good fortune to witness. When I wrote the chapter 'Compassion', you were the first person who came to my mind.

Thank you Ms Preetha Reddy, Ms Suneeta Reddy, Ms Shobana Kamineni and Ms Sangita Reddy in serving as role models of parenting. You have raised your children so well.

Thank you Simran for literally burning the midnight oil to make this book a reality. You worked hard at home in the evenings and on holidays. If it was not for your research, your suggestions and your patience, the book would have remained an idea.

Thank you Neha for managing the office with such efficiency that allowed me to take home less work on Sunday so that I could work on the book.

Thank you Prakash Iyer for encouraging me to write this book. If you had not invited me to speak at the launch of your excellent book, *The Secret of Leadership*, I would not have met Udayan and Anish, and the seed for the book would not have germinated.

Thank you Chiki and Milee for deciding to edit a book written by a first-timer even though you had so many responsibilities. Milee, your suggestions and comments gave life to this book. A big thank you from the bottom of my heart to Roshini for generously giving your time and for your prompt replies to all my queries. Your editing gave this book its soul. Thank you Mriga for copy editing the book. Your efficient and methodological approach made it so easy to work with you. A big thank you to Caroline and Shruti for organizing the launch and being such able publicists.

References

Introduction

Clark, Christina. 2012. *Children's and Young People's Reading Today: Findings from the 2011 National Literacy Trust's Annual Survey*. London: National Literacy Trust.

Federer, Roger. 2009. 'Doubles Game: Federer—My Life with the Twins'. www.independent.co.uk, 18 November. Retrieved from http://www.independent.co.uk/sport/tennis/doubles-game-federer-my-life-with-the- twins-5507567.html

Obama, Barack. 2009. 'Barack Obama: A Letter to My Daughters'. www.parade.com, 18 January. Retrieved from http://parade.com/37592/parade/barack-obama-a-letter-to-my-daughters/

Humility

PTI. 2013. '"Role Model" Sachin's Humility Makes Him Special'. *Economic Times*, 20 November. Retrieved from http://articles.economictimes.indiatimes.com/2013-11-20/news/44285098_1_sachin-tendulkar-gautam-gambhir-role-model

Beating the Odds

Foreman, Glen. 2012. 'Paralympic Archer Matt Stutzman Shows How to Fire an Arrow Without Arms'. Interview, *Perth Now*, 4 September. Retrieved from http://www.perthnow.com.au/sport/paralympic-archer-matt-stutzman-shows-how-to-fire-an-arrow-without-arms/story-fne88wsh-1226464664356

It's Never Too Late

Hiskey, David. 2011. 'Alfred Nobel Was Also Known as "The Merchant of Death"'. http://www.todayifoundout.com, 3 January. Retrieved from http://www.todayifoundout.com/index.php/2011/01/alfred-nobel-was-also-known-as-the-merchant-of-death/

Nobel Media AB. 2014. 'The Will'. www.nobelprize.org, 28 September. Retrieved from http://www.nobelprize.org/alfred_nobel/will/

Odelberg, W. (ed.). 1972. *Nobel: The Man and His Prizes*, p. 12. New York: American Elsevier Publishing Company.

Courage

Kasahara, M., K. Umeshita, Y. Inomata, S. Uemoto and Japanese Liver Transplantation Society. 2013. 'Long-Term Outcomes of Pediatric Living Donor Liver Transplantation in Japan: An Analysis of More Than 2200 Cases Listed in the Registry of the Japanese Liver Transplantation Society'. *American Journal of Transplantation* 13 (7): 1830–39.

Handling Pressure

Lawton, Kim. 2008. 'Dr. Ben Carson Extended Interview'. *Religion & Ethics Newsweekly*, 11 January. Retrieved from http://www.pbs.

org/wnet/religionandethics/2008/01/11/january-11-2008-dr-ben-carson-extended-interview/4847/

Stackelroth, Jarrod. 2008. 'Ben Carson: The Faith of a Surgeon'. HopeChannel, 1 December. Retrieved from https://www.hopechannel.com/read/ben-carson-the-faith-of-a-surgeon

Wadhwa, Nishant and Anupam Sibal. 2007. 'Recurrent Abdominal Pain among Children Attending Government and Private Schools in Delhi'. *Apollo Medicine* 4 (4): 334–38.

Making Mistakes, Accepting Flaws

Chinsky, David. 2012. 'Learning From Failure'. Posted on The Fit Leader Blog, 27 February. Retrieved from http://instituteforleadershipfitness.com/2012/02/learning-from-failure/

Gandhi, Mohandas K. 1927. *Autobiography: The Story of My Experiments with Truth*. Ahmedabad: Navajivan Trust.

Be a Dreamer

Associated Press. 2013. 'Obama to Use 2 Bibles When He Takes Oath of Office'. www.foxnews.com, 10 January. Retrieved from http://www.foxnews.com/politics/2013/01/10/obama-to-use-2-bibles-when-takes-oath-office/

King, Martin Luther, Jr. 1964. Nobel Peace Prize Acceptance Speech. Retrieved from http://www.nobelprize.org/nobel_prizes/peace/laureates/1964/king-wall.html

Lincoln, Abraham. 1858. House Divided Speech, 16 June. Retrieved from http://www.abrahamlincolnonline.org/lincoln/speeches/house.html

Miller, Dan. 2011. 'You Keep Your F—I'm Keeping My Dream!' 48days.com, 27 April. Retrieved from http://www.48days.com/you-keep-your-f-im-keeping-my-dream/

Sullivan, Bartholomew. 2013. 'Historic Connection between Barack Obama's Inauguration and Martin Luther King Day'. Scripps Howard News Service, 20 January. Retrieved from http://www.newsnet5.com/news/national/historic-connection-between-barack-obamas-inauguration-and-martin-luther-king-day

The Thirteenth Amendment. 1865. Retrieved from http://recordsofrights.org/events/120/the-13th-amendment

Find Your Calling

Honda Worldwide. 1936. 'The "Joy of Manufacturing"'. Retrieved from http://world.honda.com/history/limitlessdreams/joyofmanufacturing/index.html

Kerr, Hugh Thomson. 1994. *Famous Conversions: The Christian Experience*. Grand Rapids, MI: Wm. B. Eerdmans Publishing.

Also available on:

Reuters. 1965. 'Albert Schweitzer, 90, Dies at His Hospital'. Obituary, 'On This Day', 6 September. Retrieved from http://www.nytimes.com/learning/general/onthisday/bday/0114.html

Marshall, George N. and David Poling. 1971. *Schweitzer: A Biography*. Garden City, NY: Doubleday.

Also available on:

Reuters. 1965. 'Albert Schweitzer, 90, Dies at His Hospital'. Obituary, 'On This Day', 6 September. Retrieved from http://www.nytimes.com/learning/general/onthisday/bday/0114.html

Motorcyclemuseum.org. 2000. 'Soichiro Honda'. AMA Motorcycle Hall of Fame, Inducted in 2000. Retrieved from http://www.motorcyclemuseum.org/halloffame/detail.aspx?racerid=199

Compassion

Johnson, George D. 2011. *What Will a Man Give in Exchange for His Soul?* Bloomington, IN: Xlibris.

Making Others Happy

Chaplin, Charlie. 1940. 'The Great Dictator'. Speech in the movie, directed by Charlie Chaplin. Retrieved from http://www.charliechaplin.com/en/synopsis/articles/29-the-. Watch it on: http://www.charliechaplin.com/en/films/7-the-great-dictator/videos/1466-great-dictator-speech

————. 1954. 'Smile'. Lyrics adapted to the music in *Modern Times*. Copyright © 1954 by Bourne Co. Retrieved from http://www.charliechaplin.com/en/lyrics/articles/42-smile-lyrics

Daily Mail Reporter. 2013. 'Philanthropist Diane Disney Miller Who Inspired Her Famous Father to Create Disneyland Dies at Age 79'. Retrieved from http://www.dailymail.co.uk/news/article-2510354/diane-disney-miller-inspired-famous-father-create-disneyland-dies-age-79.html#ixzz3ldsvoi8y

Lee, Fred. 2004. *If Disney Ran Your Hospital: 9 1/2 Things You Would Do Differently*. Bozeman, MT: Second River Healthcare Press.

Wikipedia. 'Theme Parks and Beyond: 1955–66'. In 'Walt Disney'. Retrieved from https://en.wikipedia.org/wiki/walt_disney

Determination

Jobs, Steve and George Beahm. 2011. *I, Steve: Steve Jobs in His Own Words*, edited by George Beahm. Evanston, IL: Agate Publishing. Kaul, Vivek. 2009. 'What Steve Jobs Did When He Was Fired from Apple'. *DNA*, 11 May.

Giving

Carter, Christine L. 2010. 'What We Get When We Give'. *Psychology Today*, 18 February. Retrieved from https://www.psychologytoday.com/blog/raising-happiness/201002/what-we-get-when-we-give

Collins, Danica. 2014. 'The Act of Kindness and Its Positive Health Benefits'. Retrieved from http://undergroundhealthreporter.com/act-of-kindness/#axzz3qWWoPRUm

Ellick, Adam B. 2007. 'The Chicken and Rice Man'. *New York Times*, 25 November. Retrieved from http://www.nytimes.com/2007/11/25/nyregion/thecity/25dinn.html?pagewanted=all

Fleming, Stephen, C. Thomas and R. Dolan. 2010. 'Overcoming Status Quo Bias in the Human Brain'. *Proceedings of the National Academy of Sciences of the United States of America* 107 (13): 6005–09. doi:10.1073/pnas.0910380107.

Gates, Bill. 2007. 'Remarks of Bill Gates, Harvard Commencement 2007'. *Harvard Gazette*, 7 June. Retrieved from http://news.harvard.edu/gazette/story/2007/06/remarks-of-bill-gates-harvard-commencement-2007/

Post, Stephen. 2012. 'Catalyzing Happiness: Do Good; Feel Happy'. www.deliveringhappiness.com, 24 December. Retrieved from http://deliveringhappiness.com/catalyzing-happiness-do-good-feel-happy/

Rath, Tom and Jim Harter. 2010. *Wellbeing: The Five Essential Elements*. New York: Gallup Press. Retrieved from http://www.careercoachondemand.com/uploads/the_five_essential_elements_of_wellbeing_by_gallup.pdf

Tweedie, Neil. 2013. 'Bill Gates Interview: I Have No Use for Money. This Is God's Work'. *Telegraph*, 18 January.

Retrieved from http://www.telegraph.co.uk/technology/bill-gates/9812672/bill-gates-interview-i-have-no-use-for-money.-this-is-gods-work.html

Be the Change

Gangrade, K.D. 2004. *Moral Lessons from Gandhi's Autobiography and Other Essays*. New Delhi: Concept Publishing.

Gratitude

Byrne, Rhonda. 2012. *The Magic*. London: Simon and Schuster.

Pathak, Harit. 2015. 'The "Why Me?" Story by Arthur Ashe'. *Essentially Sports*, 24 May. Retrieved from http://essentiallysports.com/the-why-me-story-by-arthur-ashe/

Goals

Cavendish, Richard. 2009. 'Lee Kuan Yew Becomes Singapore's Prime Minister'. *History Today*, Volume 59, Issue 6.

Hardy, Darren. 2011. *Living Your Best Year Ever*. Dallas, TX: Success Books. Retrieved from http://www.darrenhardy.com/media/darren_hardy_-_living_your_best_year_ever_-_preview.pdf

Kennedy, J.F. 1961. 'Urgent National Needs'. Excerpt from the 'Special Message to the Congress on Urgent National Needs', Delivered in person before a joint session of Congress, 25 May 1961. Washington, DC: NASA Historical Reference Collection, NASA History Office. Retrieved from https://www.nasa.gov/vision/space/features/jfk_speech_text.html#.vixugtirliu

McCormack, Mark. 2014. *What They Don't Teach You at Harvard Business School*. London: Profile Books. Retrieved from https:// profile-business.com/media/previews/ 9781781253397_preview.pdf

Milmo, Cahal. 2014. 'Mohamed El-Erian Reveals Daughter's Talk Led to PIMCO Exit'. *Independent*, 24 September. Retrieved from http://www.independent.co.uk/news/business/us-financier-quits-2trn-investment-fund-after-his-daughter-writes-list-showing-22-life-landmarks-hed-missed-9754002.html

Yew, Lee Kuan. 2000. *From Third World to First: The Singapore Story, 1965–2000*. New York: Harper Collins.

Honesty

Bagchi, Subroto. 2010. *The Professional*, p. 15. New Delhi: Penguin Books India. Retrieved from https://books.google.co.in/books?id=tr4_endlzbcc&pg=pa15&lpg=pa15&dq=we+follow+the+ rules;+where+rules+do+not+exist,+we+use+- fair+judgment

Forgiveness

Gandhi, Mahatma. 1942. Quit India Speech, 8 August. Retrieved from http://inc.in/in-focus/249/quit-india-speech-by-mahatma-gandhi

Johnson, Scott. 2012. 'Robben Island: A Monument to Courage'. *Smithsonian Magazine*, 2 May. Retrieved from http://www.smithsonianmag.com/travel/robben-island-a-monument-to-courage-62697703/?no-ist

Mandela, Nelson. 1995. *Long Walk to Freedom*. New York: Little, Brown and Company.

Pettinger, Tejvan. 2013. 'Biography of Nelson Mandela', Oxford, www.biographyonline.net, 7 December. Retrieved from http://www.biographyonline.net/politicians/nelson-mandela.html